STOP MARKETING, START SELLING

Your guide to doubling online leads,
customers, and revenue

SHAUN TINNEY & JON MACDONALD

Edited by Neil Sniffen

Printed in the United States of America

First Printing, 2015

Printed Words Publishing
printedwordspublishing.com

ISBN-13: 978-0692503003 (Printed Words Publishing)
ISBN-10: 0692503005

The recommendations in *Stop Marketing, Start Selling* come from the experiences of our clients as we have worked with them on the problems and opportunities that they have faced. Every situation is unique, but the strategies and recommendations discussed in this book are useful for a broad variety of companies, challenges, and goals. That said, there is no guarantee that the recommendations in this book will deliver results every time. We recommend working with your team and trusted advisors as you identify and implement the strategies described herein. We cannot offer any sort of guarantee that these strategies will work for your company's situation, and we cannot be held liable for any negative outcomes that result from employing the strategies described.

Acknowledgements

This book would not have been possible without contributions from the many creative thinkers, risk takers, and caring team members who have worked at The Good to make the web a better place for all of us.

A special thank you, in no particular order, to Samuel Hulick, Shelby White, Pippa Sowers, Tom Pritchard, Laura Fischer, Larry Beal, Kerwin Carambot, Andy Baudoin, Dabe Alan, and Jason McCoskery. Especially worth recognition is Neil Sniffen, who made major contributions to getting this book into its current form, and whose editing and patience along the way made it all possible.

There have been several advisors and mentors who have supported our journey at The Good, all of whom have contributed to our success, especially Michael Bosworth, Robb Crocker, Gower Idrees, Bruce Kerr, and Steve Marsh.

Shaun would like to thank other important people along the path, including Mark Koenigsberg, David Lowe-Rogstad, and Stephen Landau. Special thanks also go to his wife, Jenn, for her constant support and encouragement throughout this journey.

Jon would like to recognize his wife, Laurel, for providing daily support, patience, and unconditional love, as well as those in EO Portland and his EO Forum who have been instrumental to his growth and success.

– Shaun Tinney & Jon MacDonald

Contents

Stuck Zone™ 3: Channel 71

Stuck Zone™ 4: Content 99

Stuck Zone™ 5: Technology 123

Foreword

Bill Murray's character in *Groundhog Day* awakens every morning stuck in the same day. In an effort to escape (or save his sanity), he performs some minor action to alter the timeline, but when he wakes the next morning it's still Groundhog Day. This happens until he learns from his mistakes, makes major changes – spoiler alert! – falls in love, and breaks the cycle.

Most of the brands I've worked with are stuck, repeating the same mistakes over and over again with their ecommerce business, not knowing what to do next. How should they grow sales? Where should they spend their money? What do their consumers want? How can they know if a particular idea is right?

Unfortunately, they don't have the benefit of starting over every day.

Fortunately, you don't need to start over. Because all of your questions have the same answer: monitor, adapt, evolve, repeat.

While I was the head of digital marketing at Easton Sports, I convinced the C-staff that using The Good's Conversion Growth Program™ was the best way to break us out of our cycle of sameness. In the first three months we saw:

- Conversion rate skyrocket by improving our product filtering interface

- Consumer engagement rise by adding videos to support our top-selling products

- Customer service issues plummet thanks to an

improved user experience

- Bounce rate drop radically by improving product content

- Mobile revenue increase more than 600%

- Total online revenue increase by more than 60%

Reporting these numbers was a big exhale moment. We finally got the results I knew were possible with the right approach. But the real celebration wasn't until a year later at our annual marketing recap, when I got to say, "Our online ad spend is outperforming last year's by 800% and our total online revenue has increased by over 170%!"

And then I dropped the mic.

OK, actually there wasn't a mic, and we were in a boardroom, but that's how I felt.

If you are willing to try the approach outlined in this book, the benefits you'll see are vast. The Good are truly generous to be sharing this knowledge with all of us, so pay attention, and you too will get to report some mic-drop-worthy numbers.

—*Stephen Lease, Founder, Simplify & Go*
Former Head of Digital & Brand Marketing at Easton-Bell Sports

Introduction

The Internet is the ultimate disrupter. It has completely altered the way we live, work, shop, and communicate. The pace at which old ways have been replaced and then replaced again with new ways is astonishing and unprecedented. In the last twenty years, we have seen landlines replaced with smartphones, post mail replaced with email, and *Mad Men*-style marketing and advertising replaced with self-service ecommerce. The new ways do not take over immediately; the disruption they introduce builds slowly until they become the only way.

One area for which this disruption has stalled is business. For most businesses that sell online or generate sales leads online, there has been a reluctance to acknowledge the new way. This book aims to reduce this reluctance and to accelerate the pace of change.

With a few notable exceptions, most business websites today are a nightmare for consumers and customers. Old methods seem to flourish on company websites with self-aggrandizing content, miserable customer experiences, and a head-in-the-sand view toward the inevitable future, a future that puts customers first.

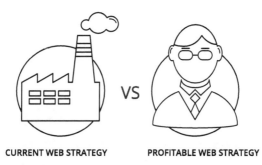

CURRENT WEB STRATEGY   PROFITABLE WEB STRATEGY

Current business website strategy	Profitable business website strategy
• Brand-centric • Poor quality content • No user testing • Marketing mindset	• Customer-centric • Regularly updated • Optimized for user goals • Service mindset

What is The Good?

The Good (thegood.com) is an ecommerce and lead generation advisory that helps brands exponentially grow their online sales. We've spent years developing, testing, and improving methods to increase conversion rates and grow revenues online. There are plenty of references to "we" throughout this book, and wherever they are, we're referring to The Good.

Whom this book is for

This book outlines a path to successful ecommerce site design and optimization. The strategies and tactics discussed are equally applicable to all lead generation sites. For the sake of simplicity, we have chosen to use ecommerce terminology throughout. Apart from not having a checkout process, the basic proposition of a lead generation site is essentially the same as that of an ecommerce site: provide value by helping people do the things they want to do. Whether you run an ecommerce or lead generation site, this book will help you grow your revenues by better understanding and serving your prospects and customers.

Serving customers

The future of effective web design (and profitable websites) begins with your customer. Creating web experiences that save them time will earn you more money. First, however, you have to know who they are, what they want, and how best to serve it to them. Much of this can be accomplished via trial and error: applying new features and tactics and making adjustments based on how these perform. Through constant iteration, you can turn a poor website into gold and avoid the expensive and often futile cycle of redesigning your entire site every few years.

> **It is hard to know what's going to make the most impact, so the ability to test and prototype with support from leadership is immensely important. If you want to succeed online, you have got to be able to take risks without being afraid to fail."**
>
> Stephen Lease, Founder, Simplify & Go and Former Head of Digital & Brand Marketing at Easton-Bell Sports

Solving your website's problems will not happen with just a new design or a fresh coat of paint. The problems are more systemic, yet they are fixable. The approach this book takes is to show you how you can take a site that is underperforming and turn it into a one that generates revenue through a process of continual learning and optimization. The best part of this approach is that, for every dollar you invest in your site to improve it for your customers, they will invest more of their money with you.

Clearing common roadblocks

The ultimate goal of the strategies and tactics outlined in this book is to guide you to help your customers get what they want from your site quickly and easily, thereby increasing the likelihood they will return in the future. To do this, there are many unseen obstacles between a company and its customers that must be removed. We will help you identify and overcome these roadblocks.

Many companies still treat their website like a commercial or mail catalog: an opportunity to capture their customer's attention and hopefully some of their cash. This is the old way of doing things, a holdover from the print and network television era of advertising that is not effective online, but still pervades the corporate mindset. A website is not a place to capture your customer's attention; it is a place to give attention to your customers. Nobody watches television for the commercials, and nobody is at your website to check out your marketing, despite what your marketing department or agency may tell you. The web is not a commercial; it is an intimate, self-service experience for which customers volunteer by opting in.

The web does not welcome the old way of thinking because that is counterproductive to the future of commerce and leads to the creation of bad websites, frustrated customers, and lost revenues. The solution is to understand your customers and give them what they want, or, at the very least, get out of the way. Nobody visits your site without a reason for doing so. Every customer visits with predetermined goals in mind, and the job of your site is to help each customer accomplish these goals.

A process for conversion growth

After years of working to create the perfect model for ecommerce and lead generation websites, we have captured the philosophy, process, and tactics that have allowed us to deliver double-digit return on investment for our clients consistently. The results we have achieved have been hard won through trial and error, leading to a process that offers companies flexibility, rapid learning, and constant iteration toward better website performance. We have honed this process over the years into what we call the Conversion Growth Program™ (thegood.com/program).

What is a Stuck Zone™, and what are Stuck Points™?

When customers cannot find what they are looking for on your site, or it is hard for them to accomplish a goal, they are stuck. When your customers are stuck, so is your revenue. The Stuck Zones™ in this book are designed logically to group a series of common obstacles, which we call Stuck Points™, in a way that makes them easier to solve. We have organized this book around these Stuck Zones™ and laid our book out to mirror a customer's journey from research to purchase or action on your brand site.

There are seven zones. The first four zones provide the baseline for creating a process and vision and lay the foundation for a healthy, growing site. The last three zones put it all together and help you craft a Conversion Growth Program™ uniquely tailored to your site and its customers.

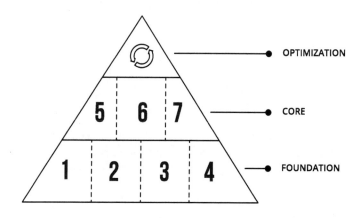

How to get the most out of this book

The first step is to get your Stuck Score™ at StuckScore.com before you begin to read. The Stuck Score™ will provide you with a baseline for optimization and help you better evaluate your site as you work your way through the book.

Once you have your baseline score, we recommend starting in Zone 1 and progressing through each chapter in order. Use the key outcomes checklists at the end of each zone to ensure that all the right pieces are in place. By working your way through each zone and checklist, you will end up with a solid foundation for your own sustainable Conversion Growth

Program™.

The process of continual learning and optimization that we use to unlock revenue from these zones for our clients has been battle tested with brands large and small. We do not claim to have all the answers, but the strategies outlined in the following chapters will help you find the right answers for your brand.

Ultimately, this book and the time and effort you invest in understanding and serving your customers will pay for themselves many times over.

1 | Brand

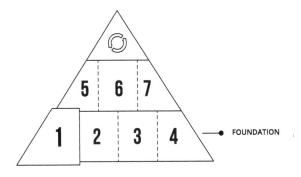

FOUNDATION

> **"** Companies must build a better experience for the future, which is online. The future is not in-store. Showrooming, fulfillment, service, and shipping might happen in-store, but physical stores are no longer the primary customer touchpoint."

Faisal Masud,
Chief Digital Officer at Staples

There is a longstanding model for using an ecommerce or lead generation website as a marketing tool to raise awareness of new products and promote brand priorities.

This model is broken.

Marketing is what drives customers to company and brand websites, not what should exist on the website. What should exist is content designed to help customers accomplish two goals: research and purchasing of products.

In this chapter, we will show you how to break out of the old brand model to start earning real revenue online and filling your pipeline with leads.

The old brand model

Most companies are organized to manufacture and deliver products across a complex supply chain. They have processes for managing production, margins, quality assurance, advertising, marketing, PR, and communications.

These processes extend to the company website that witnesses a biennial exercise in hiring a marketing agency to redesign the website completely with reckless disregard for past lessons, but with cool new features and designs.

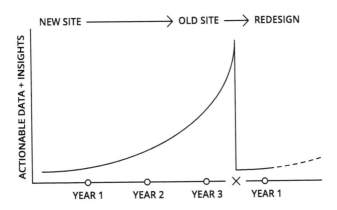

This old model lacks an effective process for managing customer service and success on the company website. This makes it nearly impossible to create or redesign a website that is relevant to customers. Ultimately, this directly affects the revenue earning potential of the website.

Current business website strategy	Profitable business website strategy
• Exists to serve the brand	• Exists to serve the customer
• Reflects the company organization, rather than being organized around customer goals	• Is built from the ground up for customer goals: research, purchase, and support
• Is not regularly tested with users	• Is constantly tested with users and regularly optimized based on findings
• Is not regularly updated to improve user experience	
• Is completely redesigned every 2-3 years from the ground up	• Has high quality content that is regularly curated to help customers get things done
• Is purchased through an ineffective Request for Proposal (RFP) process	• Has complete data tracking installed and uses regular data analysis to identify opportunities to improve experience
• Has poorly integrated technology and is hampered by regular re-platforming	• Displays and interacts perfectly on any device
• Has little to no data tracking installed, and reports on the wrong metrics	• Has simple organization and is regularly updated based on use
• Has little to no inventory management	• Is optimized continually for design, content, and navigation improvements
• Is supported only by a company's marketing budget	• Has a dedicated budget and dedicated staff to support customers and manage site content and inventory
• Is understaffed by over-tasked people	• Has a team that regularly connects with customer service to improve site content and functionality

The new brand model

The ultimate goal of the new model is to have a company's digital marketing team completely focused on ensuring that everything goes right for its customers online.

If the team understands what the company's customers are trying to accomplish online, it can spend its time solving for customer Stuck Points™ along that path.

Websites organized around the customer convert more often and make more money. However, obtaining an internal buy-in that supports a budget for a customer-centered website is not easy.

Your company may move slowly when it comes to changing budgets and hiring staff to support the website even when such a goal is clearly necessary.

Even as a team of one, however, you can use the tools in this chapter to make positive change happen.

Here are solutions to common Stuck Points™ (places on your site where visitors become stuck) when moving from the old to the new brand model.

LACK OF FUNDING TO MANAGE THE SITE PROPERLY

Even if the management at your company has an old way of thinking about the web, it will certainly be up to date on the main business goal for a website: earning increased revenue.

It is much easier to get alignment with initiatives to grow high-margin revenues than it is to get buy-in for customer research. Fortunately, there are enough cheap ways to gather the data you will need to grow revenues. Once you can demonstrate new revenue, you can win support for a larger monetary initiative.

Setting proper budgets for digital

Many companies struggle to set proper digital budgets because they have no historical patterns on which to base their budgeting decisions. The best approximation that exists comes from the print- and media-buying world. Unfortunately for everyone, these streams are not applicable in the digital realm. Once a product catalog ships or a commercial airs, that project is complete. It has been produced and exposed to the public. There is no ongoing maintenance or interaction that takes place. The web is almost exactly the opposite.

Quality Print Media	Quality Digital Media
• Photography and assets are created once	• Photography is continually updated for both a site and its products
• Copy written and flowed into layout once	• Copy constantly written, clarified and re-written based on multiple factors
• Designed, printed, and shipped on repeating seasonal cycles	• Designed and optimized continually to improve performance and customer experience

A brand's website is a business unit, and it should be run like one. It cannot thrive starving off the scraps of the marketing budget. To generate any kind of profit, a site must have its own dedicated operations budget, not just for standard development and maintenance, but for continual improvement in the name of customer service and driving conversion to boost your bottom line.

Your website is no longer a marketing tool

Why do websites tend to fall under the marketing budget in the first place? Because websites used to be used for marketing. However, customers, devices, and expectations have evolved, while most brand strategies have stood still. Digital budgets are currently structured to produce websites like print catalogs—to create a particular look and feel and to translate available content to fit into the design that everyone has internally agreed best represents the brand at that time. Then, a few years later, when nobody felt the site represented the brand look, feel, or messaging, the site was redesigned or rebuilt. Meanwhile, during the time between redesigns, the site was left idle to grow stale. Such an approach succeeds only in wasting money (possibly significant amounts) every few years, but it does not improve conversion rates, customer retention, loyalty, or profitability.

Why online sales are not a priority right now

"But wait," you say. "We do not focus on sales online because it upsets our dealers." We hear you. So-called "channel conflict" is an issue, but it is not as big an issue as you may think it is.

For one thing, you already sell online. Therefore, if your current website is disappointing your customers, customer knowledge of a poor website trickles down to your dealers and your brand. When your site makes it difficult for your customers to buy directly from you, it reflects poorly upon your brand, resulting in customer frustration and a reluctance to purchase from you either online or in stores.

Brand teams can react much faster than retailers can by leveraging campaigns, content updates, and customer experience improvements. Retailers need to plan and cannot pivot easily. Brand teams can tap into the pulse of the online market right now via their sites and use that data to build campaigns and content that will be even more relevant now and in the future. This just requires an investment in improvement.

So, invest money in making the site look great, work well, and help people buy from you. Turn your site into an asset that provides an ROI far beyond page views and Facebook likes. The only way to free up your team to generate revenue through your site is to support that effort directly, with a budget devoted to a revenue stream that creates its own positive feedback loop.

The positive feedback loop of investing in ecommerce

The expectation that results should be immediate needs to be challenged. It takes time to learn what will work best for your customers. This makes pitching every initiative as a spend-versus-return equation feel risky at first, but such initiatives become winning propositions when you learn how to focus on choosing the ideas that will benefit your customers the most. Focus on getting buy-off internally with a short-term focus on testing and learning so that your long-term profits can grow exponentially.

The more you invest in your ecommerce site, the more revenue, profit, and commerce will result. The more you invest in improving your conversion rate, the more you will earn and learn from each visitor to your site. Increasing your site's sales at higher margins means more free cash flow to invest in driving more relevant traffic. More customers, more conversions, and more revenue create a self-funding cash positive feedback loop.

Start treating your website like the self-funding business it really is. Free your website from the neglect it suffers under the marketing budget, and invest directly in the one channel that can pay for itself, quickly.

Maximizing ROI

Be clear on what a high performing brand site is supposed to do and exactly how it does it. Your website is a business asset. It is an employee of your company, a digital sales rep whose job it is to help guide and serve your current and potential customers. It has two objectives: to help customers with the research and evaluation process and to guide them to purchase. It does this via content designed to inform and ultimately increase sales.

To get a sense of where to beef up or reallocate digital budgets in the coming year, consider our top five indicators of brand website value.

1. Site content and performance

The content on your site is either converting visitors into buyers, helping current customers, or turning them both away. Evaluating content performance is rooted in understanding customer goals and tracking how the site helps them accomplish these goals. Two ways to uncover this are through analytics (evaluating pages with high exit or bounce rates) or by directly involving your customer service team.

Analytics and customer service team feedback are key to developing a clear process for identifying ineffective content that is costing money in lost sales so you can revise or eliminate it. You also will want to make sure your category structure matches the way consumers approach your products. In addition, do not forget to evaluate your product detail page content, namely, determining whether all of the most important and differentiating information is clear and easy to understand.

"Important and differentiating" does not mean pulling forward marketing jargon that effectively makes all products sound like they are the best at everything for any situation. What customers really want to know is what exactly your product is good at, how it will help them, and how it compares to other, similar products in order to make a confident, informed purchase.

2. User experience

Your brand site is a major touchpoint that consistently moves consumers closer to or further from your brand. If customers have a bad experience on your site, 90% will not return, and their feelings about your brand will not be good either. Simply put, you cannot risk providing anything less than an excellent digital experience.

Keys to being able to offer a good experience are:

- Understanding what your current and prospective customers want from your site
- Tracking unique purchase indicators and tailoring your content to each customer
- Ensuring the site is easy to use and representative of the brand

3. Performance benchmarks

When it comes to speed on the web, time really is money. Lower site load times lead to higher conversion rates. The mobile and tablet experiences are especially sensitive in this area. If you have only designed for desktop computers on fast connections, you are already losing market share to brands that are better prepared for all traffic.

Additionally, redesigning a site to look new and flashy may net a temporary 10% bump in time on site stats, but in order to see significant, long-term performance increases, you will need to serve all browsing devices through responsive design.

Finally, constant optimization leads to consistent improvement. It is critical to pay attention to site performance and to make things better, such as with benchmark speed and site performance, and identifying multi-screen enhancement opportunities. You would not plant a garden and expect it to grow without water. Optimization is the water that enables your site to grow continuously in its ability to help customers and increase revenue.

4. Search engine positioning

If you are not on Google, you do not exist. Most brands rank highly for their branded terms but are missing huge sales potential by not showing up for terms used by consumers in research mode. For example, one thing that can keep brands from ranking well for top keywords is focusing too much on tracking with what competitors are saying.

What you can do: Review on-site search terms versus organic keywords and see where you can improve, curate, or create content to help your customers and potential customers get answers to their questions. People rely on brand websites for trusted information from the source. Thus, do everything you can to be that trusted source of information and content for your brand, industry, vertical, and community.

That said, try not to be caught up in the search engine optimization game. Remember that what the search algorithms are trying to do is help people find what they are looking for. If you create quality content that answers questions and helps customers make decisions, you will be ranked appropriately when someone searches for a product in your category.

5. Social media effectiveness, reach, and approach

In social media, the most important thing brands can do is to be authentic.

That means that when things go wrong with your products or services, and customers speak out on social media, your brand has to participate actively on both sides of the conversation. This means not only recognizing but also acknowledging opportunities to serve customers better, whether this means replacing a faulty product or touting a success story.

Evaluate your current approach and your organizational structure for their service to customers through social media. Are you passively pushing out links, photos, and brand storytelling material, or do you have someone deeply connected with your customer base, interacting in real time?

Gain an edge on your competition

Make sure your brand is a few steps ahead of rather than behind your customers when it comes to providing the content they are looking for in the way they are trying to find it. Increasingly, this means video content delivered on mobile or tablet devices. It also means offering access to helpful user reviews, high-quality photos, and descriptive content that differentiates products.

Make sure digital content is more than just a checkbox on a long list of budget items because customers have already made the shift. They want everything on demand. Whether it is instant streaming or same-day delivery, be prepared to serve up what your customers are looking for when and where they want it so that your brand does not lose them to someone who will.

NOT ENOUGH STAFF OR OVERSTRETCHED RESOURCES

It is incredibly common that only a few people are responsible for managing an entire company website. Often the staff can be only one or two people. This is because companies do not understand how to hire for digital yet. A quick search of available job postings shows that most companies are looking for someone to run their website, but the combination of skills they are hoping to find is completely unrealistic.

Once in the role, the new hire is typically handed a stack of performance metrics that have little to nothing to do with increasing revenue. Often the list is nothing more than the result of a Google search of top metrics to track.

With no clear vision of what the role should be or what its occupant should do with a list of arbitrary metrics to improve, it becomes almost impossible to be an effective digital brand manager. As a result, it is easy to focus on the things that will get praise within the company. Helping customers succeed online falls by the wayside because the digital brand manager is spending time chasing down internal company priorities.

There is a better way, but it takes guts to achieve. The safest way to initialize this path is to lean on objective data to prove that the time of the digital brand manager is much better spent serving customer needs rather than the company's.

With a few wins, the manager will be able to outline a plan

either to hire additional staff or to hire specialist partners that can help drive even stronger revenue growth.

The road to success

It does not take much to succeed online. A very small team complemented by agency partners can accomplish anything. They need the right process and the right support internally. The right process involves continual learning, and the right support means a willingness to take small risks in the short term for the sake of long-term success.

In many cases, whether a brand is large or small, the brand team we work with is small. We have helped these small, internal digital teams become more effective through better execution with a process focused on their customers.

Typically, one person leads the charge for multiple initiatives by working with best-in-class partners to produce effective marketing, content assets, and a customer-goal optimized site. Client teams with the best results usually have full buy-in from their management to test new initiatives and make rapid changes to the site content based on the results of user testing and/or data analysis.

ONE-STOP SHOP AGENCY PARTNERS CANNOT DO IT ALL

For the sake of simplicity, many companies choose an agency or vendor who claims to "do it all," a one-stop shop. For the sake of revenues, many agencies and vendors make this claim. The problem is that the claim is false. They cannot do what they say, at least, not very well.

Traditional agencies focus primarily on marketing. They are qualified to design a website that looks great, but their focus is on the brand's goals and not the consumers'. The result is a site that hits all the right notes with the marketing team but sounds flat to the consumer.

Emerging solutions

Many businesses are beginning to recognize the limitations of one-stop shops and are searching for better solutions. We see two as possibilities:

1. Hire an in-house team to manage external partners and experts hired to design and develop solutions the team has created to help customers on your site.

2. Hire multiple best-in-class specialists, an approach with a number of benefits. However, getting multiple specialists to work together on a single project efficiently can be difficult. Often, the result is a disjointed finished product that requires further work (and more specialists) to resolve.

Bringing in an outside expert

An outside expert can provide the fuel needed to light up the issues needing attention and finally get them on your boss' radar. Bringing in an outside party enables you to borrow their credibility and gain an indirect third-party endorser for your plan, increasing the chances your boss will give the green light. This is simple (irrational) psychology.

Francesca Gino, author of *Sidetracked*, sums up best why paid advice is received better:

"When you pay for advice, whether it is from a doctor, lawyer, or business consultant, you can be confident that you are accessing expert information. Yet my research shows that we are not especially focused on the quality of the advice for which we pay. Rather, the cost of the advice weighs more heavily in our decisions, even when free advice is of the same quality."

Advice that is paid for is perceived as better, even if it is the same advice you have already provided. Maddening!

An outside expert provides gravitas for your existing ideas. Working with an expert can often result in getting the boss's approval for the very same idea as yours. The irony is that, by spending money on an expert, you can actually loosen the purse strings for a digital marketing initiative. If you are tired of banging your head on the wall, it is time to stop and bring in an expert.

Determine your end goal

What do you want to have at the end of the project? A new website? A new digital partner? Improved SEO? Higher conversion rates on your ecommerce site? Determine what the end goals are before you do anything else.

Begin planning the initiative

Begin planning the initiative and outlining the steps that need to occur before the initiative begins, what needs to happen while the initiative is being implemented, and how you are going to measure the results. This activity should function like brainstorming and should not yet be constrained by any real limitations. Once you have your ideas in place, organize them into a plan that seems realistic and plausible.

Prepare for objections

You know your boss best. Put yourself in their place and make lists of every potential obstacle and pitfall you can think of (e.g., budget costs, time restraints, limited knowledge base). Now come up with answers and a plan for fixes or ways around those obstacles. Sometimes there is no way around a problem, but you have now been thorough enough that you can answer these objections quickly.

Find your expert

Discover who does what you need done. You will find

a plethora of consultants and agencies that are available to respond to your call. Do some research on the most interesting ones to see where they speak, what they write, who their clients are, and what industries they specialize in. Once you find someone who is an expert in the area of your project and in your industry, make contact.

Coordinate with your expert

Be upfront with your expert, and lay out your end goals, your plan, and any obstacles you see as potential obstructions. The expert should be willing to work with you to move the initiative in the right direction while providing input and recommendations for any needed course corrections. This is also the time to ask the expert how much it will cost to implement your idea. It is a question your boss will ask.

It is show time

First, check your ego at the door. This is the hardest part for some people, but letting the expert be the person who discusses the idea and the plan is essential for this approach to work. You have hired them for this purpose. Let them explain your idea, the reasoning behind it, and the ROI. Remember, by bringing in this outside expertise you are actually promoting yourself and advancing your ideas.

Follow-up and planning for the project

The last step is also the beginning of the next phase. You will need to close the deal with your boss. Once the boss signs off, you can move into the planning phase for your project.

Bringing in an outside expert is one of the best ways to convince executives that something needs to happen. Therefore, if your head hurts from running into the brick wall of "No!" too many times, find yourself a good, sturdy expert who will help you scale the wall instead.

STUCK POINT™ 4:

MITIGATING INVESTMENT RISK

To minimize real investment risk, you must change the entire process of creating and maintaining websites. Instead of redesigning the site from the ground up, implement a continuous cycle of improvement.

Rather than spending a few hundred thousand dollars every few years for a brand new website that may or may not be relevant to customers, invest a few thousand dollars each month to keep the site relevant to ever-changing consumer needs.

There are specific places on your site to invest time and effort that will quickly provide a return. Uncovering these key areas can be as simple as digging into your site analytics to find the top 20% of site usage. Using this data can help make small changes to the site that result in large revenue gains. Ultimately, this approach can save a company millions in redesign costs.

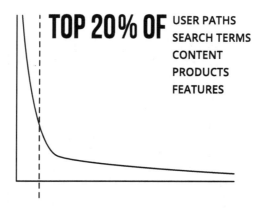

If your company insists on completely redesigning its website every few years, make sure that you leverage the site's past failures and all the data collected during its term of use to inform the design of the new site. Without a deep understanding of why the site failed to work before, it is impossible to create a site that solves those problems now.

STUCK POINT™ 5:

INTERNAL DEPARTMENTS FIGHTING FOR SITE SPACE

Your ecommerce website is never the place for internal departments to post content, unless that content aligns with the overall strategy of creating a site that helps customers research and purchase products.

To bolster this argument, consider Google. The Google homepage is the epitome of understanding visitor goals and helps visitors do exactly what they came to Google.com to do: search. Google does not win the search engine wars because it convinces everyone it has the best algorithm; Google.com wins because it only tries to do one thing really well.

Even at Google, however, there is someone who must defend that homepage every day from the creeping expanse of the Google universe. Every brand site needs a champion to stand firm and keep the site's focus on serving its customers. Be like Google. Make sure that the one thing you do well is helping your customers with their goals on your site.

Getting buy-in

Many executives still have no clue what a person in a digital role does. They will not necessarily know exactly what needs to be done, but they will trust their people to do it. Some executives do not know what to do, and it scares them. They are afraid of making mistakes. The digital world feels foreign, so it is difficult for them to relate to it. They know it is important, but they do not know how to support it.

By default, average executives or leaders assume that they know everything they need to know. They assume that the way things work now is pretty much the way they used to work, just with more buzzwords.

Five years ago, a great email campaign was a sure bet for generating traffic. Today, email does not achieve nearly the same level of traction. There is no longer a single clear path to success on the web. There is never going to be just one thing that you can do well in order to succeed. It will be twenty different things. It is hard to know what will to make the most impact, but the ability to compare and test prototypes without being afraid to fail and with support from company leadership is immensely important. The companies that do not give their digital teams the ability to fail in the short term are going to fail in the long term.

STUCK POINT™ 6:

GOALS AND KPIs MAKE NO SENSE FOR THE BOTTOM LINE

Site analytics are critical to the evaluation and oversight of a website, but they can also be a site's downfall.

Far too often, brands become mired down in the weeds of analytics, focused on the wrong numbers or not fully understanding what the right numbers mean. This inaccurate focus and limited understanding creates little to no value and often results in an expensive redesign. Such results are an avoidable waste of money.

Here are some of the most common metrics terms and their meanings on which corporate executive misplace their focus.

Bounce rate

When a visitor arrives on your site and leaves without viewing additional pages, that classifies as a bounce. The frequency with which this happens is your bounce rate. A high bounce rate usually indicates that most of the potential customers who visited a particular page did not find what they were looking for and immediately exited the page to go to a competitor's site.

High bounce rates can happen for a variety of reasons. Uncovering those reasons will help decrease the bounce rate. Some of the usual offenders include:

- Traffic driven from the site because of an ad that promised something the site failed to deliver
- Too many marketing tactics employed on one page, overwhelming the viewer
- Social media feeds putting irrelevant content front and center
- Email pop-ups obstructing a visitor or presenting offers that do not resonate
- Auto-rotating banners that distract visitors with irrelevant content

Look at the tactics and content employed on your pages with high bounce rates. If you see any from this list, you will want to fix them.

The bottom line is that a high bounce rate is not the end of the world, but does indicate a page is wasting your money by repelling hard-won clicks. Fine-tuning the content and understanding the sources of the page traffic can help remedy a high bounce rate.

Time on site (or average session duration)

At first glance, many people think of time on site as a metric that needs to increase. It seems logical that the longer someone spends on your site, the better that site's content must be. This is not always the case. A site with positive revenue growth and low time on site actually indicates a very healthy site. It indicates that customers are able to find what they are looking for quickly, purchase it, and get back to their busy lives.

The bottom line is that we have consistently seen reduced time on site go hand-in-hand with increased conversion rates and higher order values. By simplifying the content and navigation structure of the website based on customer goals, we help customers find what they are after faster so they may buy more often.

Page views

Page views and time on site are metrics with similar implications. That customers are spending their time clicking around your site. However, this metric is meaningless to your site's revenue.

It is a "feel good" metric that can also indicate a negative trend. If customers are viewing many pages, but not purchasing, your site is failing to do what you want it to do.

In general, the fewer clicks it takes for someone to find what they came for, the more likely it is that they will come back in the future.

Conversion rate

Conversion rate is an indicator of how effectively your site closes sales. Many factors influence conversion rate including navigation, content, and mechanics. Improving this rate takes time as it requires persistent site testing and iteration.

The trouble with conversion rate, as with any other single metric, is that myopic focus on it will prevent you from seeing the whole picture (or in many cases, the whole problem). Track your conversion rate, set a target goal for how far you want to move the needle, but do not let it be the only metric in your view.

Remember that metrics are always lagging indicators that do not capture the whole picture of the customer experience. It is easy to become bogged down in dashboards looking at graphs, when you need to be focused on what the experience is like for a potential customer who visits your website and tries to accomplish something.

Dealing with company management

Executive teams have varying degrees of understanding when it comes to creating a compelling customer experience in digital media. It is hard for c-level executives to wrap their heads around the website as a product; they tend to think of it more like a catalog or a dealer finder. That is a misunderstanding of the potential impact that the digital experience can have for a product, service, or company.

This leads to management thinking they have really great ideas that have actually been really terrible ideas for about seven years. The further away they are from the front lines, the less able executives are to connect with the consumer. This can make it a struggle to justify the cost and explain the benefit of building a great customer experience online.

There is also an inaccurate sense of how long it takes to complete digital projects. Nobody believes things should take a long time because there's "out of the box" stuff out there, and they see marketing turn things around quickly. They are accustomed to a world where timeline expectations are short, budgets are small, and requirements are high.

Executive teams often do not believe it takes as long and costs as much as it really does to finish a digital project. Thus, they impose arbitrary deadlines and budgets, that cause their team to figure out what they can get done by that certain date or with that certain budget, rather than allowing the site to be properly developed for a great customer experience (and higher revenues).

The key thing to help executive teams see is that they would not put these same unrealistic expectations on creating a physical product. Just because the end-product is digital does not mean that it takes any less time or effort to create. The idea that you can just get some digital people in a room and give them a bunch of

Red Bull to launch a site quickly is ridiculous because you need customer interaction with the site in order to improve it, perfect it, and make it produce expected revenue. Companies have learned a lot about the mistakes of rushing a physical product, but often do not realize that the same pitfalls apply to digital projects.

> **Leadership tends to have a print-minded view of the web: refine until perfect, then distribute. The web is the opposite: distribute, then continually refine."**
>
> Ken Soliva, Senior User Experience Designer at Design Concepts

Digital brand managers get caught up in conversations about digital initiatives rather than aggressively pursuing an understanding of the ongoing results of their current digital properties. They lose track of the growth potential from existing projects and get sidetracked thinking about ongoing initiatives rather than ongoing improvements.

If you outline the jobs that each of your digital tools and platforms is accomplishing for your company and your customers, it will be much easier to get buy-in on the effort and time required to create a great customer experience online. Show which approach is appropriate for which job and the time and effort it takes to do the job well, and then provide clear metrics of success focused on tying revenue gained to efforts invested.

STUCK POINT™ 7:

NO CLEAR VISION FOR YOUR WEBSITE

The purpose of your brand website is to help your customers find, research, and purchase your products. By doing this well, you improve your brand's reputation. Many companies struggle unsuccessfully to align themselves behind this purpose, condemning their websites to be vaguely useful and mostly self-serving.

At The Good, we have seen this play out in hundreds of strategy sessions we have run with brand leaders—at first, brand goals take priority over what will matter most to customers. By the end of every session, they realize that *their* goals are completely realized when the brand site helps customers accomplish *the customers'* goals.

Here are two examples of brand goals from our sessions that show how we converted them into customer (goal) solutions:

Brand Goal: Increase site revenue.
Customer Solution: Make it easier for customer to research and purchase products.

Brand Goal: Increase returning customer conversion.
Customer Solution: Personalize site for returning visitors and make it simple for returning customers to find and purchase products they are interested in quickly.

From our brand session experience, we have created a list of the most common brand goals:

1. Increase sales
   a. Direct global sales
   b. Retail sales
   c. Online sales
   d. Overall product sales
   e. Increase average total per transaction
2. Increase revenue
3. Increase lead conversions
   a. Reduce time from lead submission to purchase
4. Increase consumer engagement
   a. Increase return visits
   b. Increase new and returning site visitors
   c. Increase consumer reviews
   d. Increase dealer lookups
   e. Increase engagement from verticals to brand story
   f. Increase email newsletter and social opt-ins
5. Increase social engagement with brand
   a. Engagement, connections, active conversations
6. Increase customer touch points (including after purchase)
7. Reduce avoidable calls to customer support
8. Reduce bounce rate on homepage
   a. Increase understanding of consumer behavior online

If your brand goals are on this list, you are in good company. Some of the biggest brands in the world listed some or all of these as their brand goals. The trick for them and now for you is to use the identified brand goals and align them with your customers' goals. Succeed at that and kick your revenues into high gear.

Key outcomes checklist:

☐   Correct funding for your site

☐   Dedicated staff and partner support

☐   Focus on process (not projects)

☐   Internal support and buy-in

☐   Clear vision and brand goals

Moving forward

Your brand website can no longer be thought of as simply a marketing platform for your brand. It is a virtual store for your customers to buy directly from you.

Once your customers are onsite (and in your store), your marketing has won. Now it is time to serve your customers.

2 | Customer

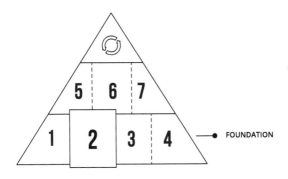

> **Most managers think that, if you put the customer first, you are putting the organization second, as if you can't achieve your organizational goals if you put the customer first. It is a false trade-off. If you really want to make lots of profit, you have to put the customer first. Businesses exist because of their customers."**

Gerry McGovern,
Author, CEO at Customer Carewords

You likely already understand what it is like to shop on a website that is not focused on helping you get what you are looking for. It is frustrating.

The trouble with shopping online is that it is overly difficult. All too frequently, it feels like running an obstacle course of pop-ups, marketing jargon, and bad content. The worst part is that, if you even make it to the shopping cart, you are asked for more personal information than when you are at a doctor's office.

By placing artificial barriers in front of customers, brands actually reduce conversion rates, annoy potential customers, and lose sales.

There is a better way.

Think of your site as a store

The job of your website is to create an excellent customer experience, to solve the problems that customers brought with them, and help them find what they are looking for quickly and easily.

To do this, think of your ecommerce website as a retail store so you can envision and create the kind of experience you want

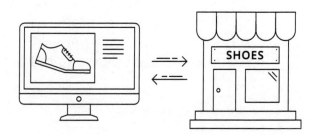

your customers to have.

It is rare to walk into a retail store and immediately be accosted by a salesperson asking for your email address. Yet many sites do this to their online customers. Retail can tell us an awful lot about how to design our sites effectively and treat our online customers. Well-trained retail staff answer questions and point customers in the right direction to help them find what they are looking for and be on their way. Your website should be no different.

Any site that sells products or services is a store. Unfortunately, for most brands, their websites are stores at which nobody would want to shop. Since the online store does not provide help from employees, it must present simple ways for customers to find and buy the right product.

Employees in a successful retail store make every effort to be helpful to their customers. They respect their customers' time and want them to leave with a good impression of their brand. That is why they were hired and how their performance is typically assessed.

Just like employees in a retail store, your website should have a clear job description to allow you to judge its success at helping your customers and your company get what they need from it.

Similar to a retail store, your website should be clearly organized around the ways that your customers expect to shop. A well-organized website will place the products that are sold the most or are responsible for the greatest revenue up front so they are readily available for customer purchase. To begin organizing your website, you first need to understand who is shopping at your online store.

NO CLEAR CUSTOMER PROFILE

One of the first questions we ask our clients when beginning a new project is, "Who buys from you online?"

If ten people are in the meeting, we will often get ten different answers. It is surprising how frequently among high-ranking decision makers in a brand there is no clear consensus on who buys from them. There are assumptions, but they often have no data to back up these assumptions.

For many brands, their website exists as an extension of their marketing with an old view that it is only a vehicle to tell the brand story. The reality is that customers are visiting the brand site not to hear about the brand (they already know about the brand; that is why they are on the site), but to research and purchase products from the brand directly.

By ignoring this fact, it is no wonder that so many brands are constantly redesigning their websites every couple of years.

To understand who your customers are and what their goals are, you will need to learn about them.

To whom do we sell?

More often than not, new client discovery sessions reveal a lack of clarity on the brand's ideal customer profile. At one meeting for a large manufacturer, the question of

"Who buys from us?" resulted in a massive whiteboard diagram connecting at least eighteen different buyer types to the brand's offering. After working through a series of questions to uncover what made each customer unique or similar, we netted a total of just two customer types. What brought about the collapse of this massive list of customer types? The overlap was not their demographic group but *their reasons for buying* the product.

One client that sells lifestyle gear has its main office in a college town. For years, the client was under the impression that college students were its primary customer type because they saw them using their product on a daily basis. Our research and analysis revealed that college students made up only 2% of the client's customer base. Over 52% of our client's customers were actually moms. While each group had similar reasons for buying the brand's product, this update in the understanding of their most active customer allowed them to tell a brand story that resonated much better with this demographic, dramatically improving conversion.

Who is your customer?

Creating an ideal customer experience starts by understanding your customer. You may be surprised to find that the person you think you are selling to is not the person who is actually buying your product. To discover your real customer, consider the basic tools for gathering that information.

GATHERING CUSTOMER INFORMATION

Customer surveys are an easy (and often free) way to gather important data about your customers. There is nothing quite like going to the source to get actionable information.

Start with the least you need to know

Before you try to gather information from your customers, start by getting a quick read on how things are going. A Net Promoter Score is a quick and simple way to do just that. The score is calculated on a scale from 1-10 by asking visitors, "How likely is it that you would recommend our company/product/ service to a friend or colleague?"

Such a survey is an excellent starting place because it provides a sense of the road ahead. You will quickly know whether you will be able to focus on smaller improvements to the customer experience, or if there are larger roadblocks that must be cleared first.

A score of 9 or 10 is excellent and suggests that relatively small improvements will go a long way to improve customer experience. A score of 7 or 8 suggests that significant roadblocks need to be removed to improve your customer experience. A score of 6 or lower offers an opportunity (in actuality, demands) to reach out directly to that customer and solve a problem for them that could transform them from a complainer to a customer.

There are a number of ways to gather this score, ranging from a simple Google Form to more robust platforms.

> 🗨🗨 People tend to believe that companies are big anonymous factories, but when you interact directly with your customers and address their concerns it is amazing to see the turnaround between people who hate you for one reason or another, and converting them into a promoter for life!"
>
> Shane Vaughn, President of Ecommerce at Snake River Farms

Gathering customer data

There are many ways to gather customer data and a number of tools to help analyze the data. We typically use SurveyMonkey (surveymonkey.com) because it is easily customizable and offers a wide array of question options, survey logic flows, and great data analysis tools. Google Forms is also a decent free alternative to a paid service, but it has no built-in analysis tools.

Other great options that allow you to purchase responses based on detailed demographic data are listed at thegood.com/tools.

Creating the survey

The survey should not take long to create, but make question design a top priority. Design each question with a specific learning goal. Ideally, the questions will reveal the individual behaviors and preferences of your customer types.

Begin with classifying questions, and make each question multiple-choice. This helps keep the survey short and allows for a detailed analysis of the survey data. There are times when a free textual response question is appropriate, but use them with caution as these questions are more difficult to analyze quickly (or at all).

When you review your questions prior to use, always check that they will help increase your understanding of customer goals with relevant, actionable information.

Here is the typology of questions we typically use to create customer surveys:

1. Segmentation question (allow customers to put themselves into a meaningful group)

2. Product ownership question (how many/which products do they own, if any?)

3. Behavior-oriented question (how do they buy/how often do they buy)

4. Content-oriented question (which content is most useful in making a purchase decision?)

5. Decision-making question (what factors are most important when purchasing: durability, style, price, etc?)

6. Goal-discovery question (what are customers trying to accomplish on your site?)

7. Goal-ranking question (which goal is most important to them, most often?)

8. Product-use question (how frequently/for what purpose do they use your products?)

9. Brand selection question (why do they buy from you: price, quality, better functionality, reputation,

recommendation, etc?)

10. Open question (what else do you need to know?)

11. Option to participate in telephone follow-up (provide their phone number to be contacted for a brief telephone interview in exchange for an incentive offer)

Distributing your survey

While it is easy to purchase survey responses from companies like Survey Monkey or Amazon Mechanical Turk, there are two free and extremely relevant channels you can use to gather responses quickly: your brand's marketing email lists and social media.

For your email marketing list, sending a quick survey to a marketing list will offer you the opportunity to connect with customers and build valuable business intelligence in the process. Because these are people you reach out to frequently, it is vital that you segment your list appropriately to minimize the number of people who opt out. Run a few content tests early on before sending out a survey to your entire list.

Three simple segmentations are engaged (opened an email in the last 180 days) or unengaged (has not opened an email in 180 days) and customer (email obtained via past purchase).

It's important to get enough responses to your survey to be able to draw confident conclusions from the data you'll receive. A quick Google search for "survey statistical significance" will turn up calculators and charts to determine how many responses you'll need to achieve statistical relevance with your survey responses.

Writing the email

The content of the survey request email should be to-the-point and free of any marketing. We have found that a plain (or minimally styled) text email with only one to two sentences works the best for getting a solid response rate. Try to be direct and grateful for the help.

Testing the subject and content of your emails before sending a final version will guarantee a greater response rate.

Here are a couple of example survey request email templates that have worked well for B2C and B2B clients.

Potential B2C Subject Lines

Help us improve our site with this brief survey
Brief survey to improve [yourbrandsite.com]
Get a 15% discount coupon by taking this survey
Take our survey, get a coupon for 15% off any purchase

Brief B2C Body Copy

Hi [Their Name],

We're updating ourbrandsite.com and could use your help! If you are interested, please take this short survey: LINK

Thanks,
Our team

If you are surveying other businesses, it can be helpful to offer to share the data with the participants, though this is not always necessary. Here is some potential copy to test:

Potential B2B Subject Lines
Share your opinion and gain industry insights
[First Name] - your opinion for our industry survey
2 minute survey on [Company Name]'s research process

Brief B2B Body Copy
Hi [Their Name],

We're conducting an industry wide survey to improve the process of _____ online.

If you will take 2 minutes to fill out the survey at [LINK], we will gladly share the results with you.

Thanks,
Our team

Sending the email

If you have been running email campaigns, you should have the timing down for when to send the email for optimal opens and clicks. If you have no idea when people are most likely to read your emails, try sending on Tuesday morning or midday Thursday.

Check out mailchimp.com/resources/research/ for some very detailed research on best send times by industry to maximize open and click rates.

Posting to social platforms

Posting on social media is a less direct interruption for your audience than sending emails, and it can be done more than once in a reasonably short period without upsetting the reader.

Repost something similar to your initial post to encourage more participation before you end the survey. Let them know you are about to stop taking responses, and you will get another rush of participants.

Writing the post

When it comes to posting on your social media accounts, the most important quality is authenticity. You have developed a brand voice that feels consistent to your followers, and this is no time to risk a break in that consistency. If you have a fun and funky approach, take a fun and funky approach to this survey request. Stay true to your brand personality.

Incentivizing responses

Many customers are willing to fill out a short survey without getting anything in return. However, if you really want to increase the number of responses, offer a reward. Discounts, free shipping, a free gift with purchase, or a gift card to Starbucks should suffice.

GATHERING CUSTOMER INSIGHT

The data you will gather from a multiple-choice survey will only paint part of the picture required to understand your customers' goals. You will also need anecdotal material to add life and individual perspective to your research. This will require you to speak with your customers directly.

The best way to gather these candidates is simply to ask for their willingness to participate at the end of the survey. This is also a great time to offer an incentive (or an additional incentive).

You will be surprised how many people are willing to include their phone number and offer to be interviewed over the phone.

Customer interviews

Once you have gathered your survey responses and you have a list of people to interview, it is important that you design questions that will fill in the gaps from the survey. Analyze survey data and look for trends and outliers that either make perfect sense or no sense at all. These are the areas in which you will be asking your customers to share their experiences with you.

Call prep

Just because someone said you could make contact does not mean it will be easy to do so. It is very important to schedule an appointment with customers to whom you plan to reach out. Send them a calendar invite in advance, and send a reminder email the day before your appointment to confirm their availability.

Some people are very easy to interview. They will do most of the talking unprompted and will offer up some incredibly valuable information, quotes, and perspectives on the site and brand. Others are more reluctant to share, requiring more prompting to elicit useful responses. Plan to conduct at least five customer interviews before you'll have a clear sense of the common anecdotal site issues.

Making the call

1. Starting things off right

When you do get on the phone with customers, it is important to make them feel as comfortable as possible. To do this, let them know that they are the experts on this call and their responses are going to be used to help the brand improve the website. Respect their time, and stick to the scheduled time for the call.

Remind the customer being interviewed that there really are no wrong answers and, even though you have a few questions you would like to ask them, you really want to understand the experiences they have had with your brand in the past, and what they like or do not like about being a customer.

2. Questions to ask

Most customers have a hard time expressing what they want or what would make them a happy customer. For this reason, it is essential to ask questions about the kind of experiences a customer has had in the past with your brand, or with another company. It is always easier for customers to talk about what has happened than to speculate.

If you want to ask a question about your website, ask customers about the experiences they have had with the website in the past:

- Was it easy to navigate?
- Did they find what they were looking for?
- Did they typically use the navigation or search box to find that they were looking for?
- Were the search results helpful?
- Was it easy to check out?
- Did they run into any obstacles or content that was confusing?

Whether you use these questions or a list of your own, it is likely that the questions will not be as relevant once the conversation gets going, but they can be a great fallback resource if other initiatives come to a dead end.

During the interview, listen and be curious about what your customers are saying. Remain open-minded as the conversation unfolds, and you will gather some great insights that will add anecdotes to the data you have gathered in response to more formal questions.

End the interview by thanking them for their time and asking for permission to follow up with additional questions via email.

If you'd rather not conduct these interviews yourself, we'd be happy to help. Email hello@thegood.com for more information about our customer research services.

LEVERAGING CUSTOMER SERVICE FEEDBACK

Your customer service team is a gold mine of information. This cannot be overstated. Unfortunately, the customer service department is usually overlooked when it comes to discovering areas to improve on the website or in a company's online content.

The goal in interviewing customer service staff is to understand the most common issues, complaints, problems, hassles, and struggles that they have listened to customers talk about with your brand and website. Their insights into customer pain points can direct your focus toward improvements that can produce immediate positive results.

Start your interview by simply asking your customer service staff to describe a typical day for them, including the most common issues they help resolve for customers. In almost every interview of a customer service team we have conducted, new and unexpected areas of pain have been exposed and old issues that continue to plague customers have resurfaced.

Here is a foundational interview script of questions for your customer service staff:

- Can you [customer service staff] walk me [interviewer] through a typical day for you?
- What are the most common requests or issues that you get?
  - Can you break down the requests by volume?

- Per product?
- Per content type?
- What are the main categories you would put customer service requests into?
- What are the most common questions or complaints you get about the website?
- Can you think of a time when individuals had trouble using the site or could not find what they were looking for?
- What are the biggest challenges customers face when buying online?
- If you could change the website to help make your job easier, what would you change?
- Have people called after visiting the site being unable to find answers to their questions?
- Do people ever say "I wish you guys / the website would ___"?
- Do you have a customer-service-specific "guiding star" that you follow?
- What are some of the ways that you explain product features to customers?
- What does _____ as a brand mean to you? What is your company all about?

Customer service interviews, which can be very informal, should become a regular part of the ongoing maintenance of your site. We call this opening the customer service feedback loop.

Opening the customer service feedback loop

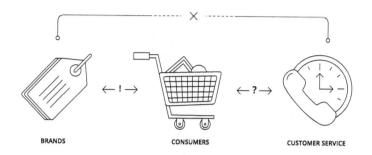

BRANDS   CONSUMERS   CUSTOMER SERVICE

To open the customer service feedback loop, initiate a dialogue between your brand's customer service and sales and marketing departments with a call log. Set up a Google Form or some other simple data capture tool so your customer service team can log a portion of their call data.

The call log should be very simple to complete (radio buttons, drop downs with preconfigured options, etc.), capturing the following information from each caller to customer service:

- Customer segment
- Product categories of interest
- Key issues prompting customer to call for help (purchasing, product info, sizing, warranty, return, shipment tracking, account log in, team purchase, etc.)
- Open text box to summarize key issues and any related notes

We have found that this simple tool is responsible for some of the most dramatic improvements in customer experience and the content of brand sites.

Some of the most common digital failures reported on call logs include:

- Technical jargon disguised as marketing copy
- Confusion caused by email failures
- Lack of useful sizing and fitting tools
- Complicated account registration or login requirements
- Poor warranty, replacement parts, and shipment tracking information

The list of issues you and your customer service team uncover may look daunting, but do not panic. To prioritize your roadmap for making site changes based on your data, focus on the top 20% of the commonly reported issues list. There will always be outliers that may require a large investment to solve, but the majority of site changes that will result from this effort will be relatively simple matters relating to the user interface (UI) and site content updates.

CLARIFYING CUSTOMER GOALS

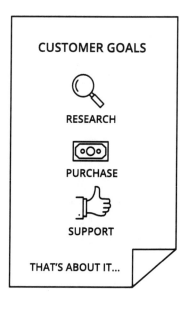

If you've completed the research exercises to this point, you should have a clear picture of your customers' goals, desires, struggles, and motivations. This list will drive decisions about site content and features.

By organizing your site's content and functionality based on a clear list of customer-defined goals, you can avoid the distractions that trap most brand sites. Use this list of goals to help decide which features and enhancements to invest in and help prevent the unintentional sabotage of customer experience.

Here is a list of customer goals, based on our research, to inspire your own list:

1. Research a product (type)
   a. Support effortless research (clear pathways)
   b. Support current customers who have specific product questions (for already purchased goods)

c. Support multiple devices (mobile, tablet, desktop)
d. Compare products/prices/features
e. Dealer or store lookup
f. Fit or size chart

2. Buy a product (and feel good about their decision)
   a. Support effortless purchase
   b. Support effortless returns (boost confidence)

3. Needs fulfillment
   a. Control
      i. Flexible return/replace a product
      ii. Research and compare seamlessly
      iii. Purchase confidence
   b. Self-expression
      i. Product customization & personalization
   c. Recognition
      i. Loyalty programs
   d. Care (Connectedness)
      i. Engage with brand content (social)
      ii. Customer support/connection with the brand

Note that each of the brand goals we have outlined can be reframed to support a customer goal. If you can help your customers reach their goals, they will help you reach yours.

Key outcomes checklist:

- ☐ Customer profile
- ☐ Customer data
- ☐ Customer stories
- ☐ Customer service data
- ☐ Clear customer goals

Moving forward

It is easy to forget that a human being is on the other side of the digital display.

Your customers are real people with real problems, and they have turned to your site for solutions. It does not matter whether your solution is a bike helmet or a vacation package, remember that the reason your website exists is to help your customers. When they recognize this—and they absolutely will—they will gladly help improve your bottom line.

3 | Channel

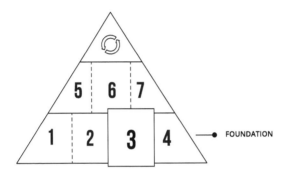

FOUNDATION

> **"** At the end of the day, the consumer expects that, no matter which channel they interact with a brand through, it will be a seamless, frictionless experience."

John Evons,
VP Global Digital Commerce at Fuerst Group

Three factors drive online revenues: traffic, average order value, and conversion rate. A factor imbalance will slow online revenue growth.

In this chapter, we look at how you can improve your site's traffic by making all your channels more efficient.

Competing sales channels

Most brands struggle to find a balance between maximizing the profitability of the products sold on their brand website and the revenue generated by their retailers, dealer networks, and distributors.

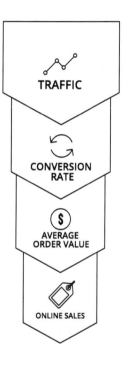

Brands report to us that channel conflict is the number one reason why they underfund, undercut, or avoid setting up an ecommerce site. There is good reason for this concern. Retail partners are genuinely worried about brands moving into the space of retailers by selling direct online, and many brands depend upon their wholesale revenue for the majority of their revenue each year. Additionally, having access to smaller retail partners allows brands more access to more customers and markets.

So the big question is: How do both the brand and its retailers win? The answer is by creating a great brand site. Here is how to tighten up all your channels so that your brand site helps all its partners.

STUCK POINT™ 1:

CHANNEL CONFLICT

Upsetting retail partners, distributors, and dealers is a real concern. They are often responsible for the majority of a brand's total revenue. However, channel conflict does not mean a brand website should be terrible at helping customers research and purchase products. In fact, the better the brand site experience is for consumers, the more likely it is they will buy (from the brand site or a partner).

Brands that succeed in overcoming channel conflict recognize that their brand site is the go-to source for product information and support.

Your site is a huge lead generator for your retail and dealer network. Providing a great brand experience makes it more likely that customers will use your site as a resource to find local businesses to buy your products.

Another solution is offering a "Buy Local Now" button on the site. While this may seem to contradict a brand's desire to capture more margin, it reflects a segment of the market that cannot wait two-to-fourteen days for a product to arrive. Parents may need to buy cleats for their child's first soccer practice that starts in two hours. Brands build loyalty by helping customers meet their needs regardless of whether the answer to that need is online or in stores. According to a 2013 Google study, 40% of sporting goods customers who used a store locator to find a retailer went into the store to make a purchase (source: Carabetta and Marchant, 2013). Armed with that information, what retailer would not want more product information and accessibility available to customers?

Once you are selling online, nobody knows how much you are selling. There's no reason to make your customers suffer through a poor online experience just to keep your retail partners from feeling threatened by a well-designed customer experience.

Brands and retailers could benefit more by focusing on creative ways to leverage their partnerships to drive more sales overall. Grow the pie, rather than trying to divide it up, and defend the pieces.

Using acronyms to our advantage

Most executives do not understand the common acronyms of the web (SEO, SEM, PPC, etc.). Some fear them, and most think they are really important. This can be used to our advantage if we are careful.

There are some simple concepts on which we can train our teams (and our executives) to focus. PPC and email are simple, easy-to-measure concepts and tools that digital marketers can use to create buy-in for the more esoteric initiatives like SEO and retargeting.

If you can demonstrate enough success through one of the easy-to-understand channels, your executive or manager will likely leave you alone "to work on that other web stuff."

ALIENATING RETAIL PARTNERS

Brands need to get creative in supporting retailers to improve relationships and create an "everybody wins" mindset. Tactics like co-branded email campaigns or custom landing pages using brand content allow brands to get their seasonal marketing messages out to their retailers' broad customer base, and retailers get help in promoting sales of a brand's product.

While it is certainly not wise to undercut your dealers with your online pricing, there are number of other ways to promote sales on your site that will essentially fly under the radar, keeping dealer relationships strong while boosting your high-margin sales online.

Here are a few tactics you can try to boost online sales without alienating your retail partners.

Exclusive products

Offer products on your ecommerce site that are exclusive to the site—uniquely designed products available only online. This can be an enhanced version of a current product, or something designed to complement a popular product that is not available elsewhere. This approach has the added benefit of creating buzz around the unique product because it can only be found in one place, avoiding channel conflict with your retail partners.

Personalized products

Product personalization is becoming easier to provide with the advent of new manufacturing techniques. Nike ID led the way and demonstrated the strong demand for personalized products that can only be purchased directly from the brand. Nike shoes are available at many retailers, but you can only get a customized version of Nike shoes through their website or the Nike Store.

Whether you offer customized colors, personalized printing, laser etching, or any other way to personalize products, this approach offers a powerful way to overcome channel conflict while increasing product margins.

Product giveaways

Everyone loves the BOGO (buy one, get one). This timeless tactic creates an immediate sense of value for your customer. By using this tactic, you can create value for your consumer and increase sales for your brand. This tactic does not undercut your retailers, because you are not lowering the price of your products, only increasing the value of purchasing directly from you. In this way, you are able to provide a discount without actually discounting your price.

Bundles and kits

Product bundles and kits are a helpful way to bring new customers into the brand and keep customers coming back.

Whether it is a new baby diaper bundle, a snowboard package, or back-to-school supplies, creating bundles and kits for your products can promote increased sales, help customers, and allow product discounts without direct price competition on individual products.

Increasing average order value

We helped one client increase their average order value from $97 to over $150 through strategic bundling of their most popular products. The strategy works well all year long, but is especially effective during the holiday shopping season.

We ran multiple tests of bundle promotions, merchandising, and placement. When bundled products were combined with shipping incentives, average order value increased significantly, because the order total required to unlock free shipping was set slightly higher than the most popular bundle prices.

Free shipping

Offering free shipping allows your brand to offer products at a reduced cost without actually undercutting your retail partners. Companies like Zappos have built an entire customer base on making shipping and returns free and easy.

Free shipping offers can increase the average order value. Setting the threshold for free shipping just above the average price of the brand's products is often enough incentive for customers to add one more item to their cart. Free shipping also positively influences a large portion of the revenue puzzle, namely, conversion rates.

Tactics to avoid

Overcoming retailer fears about direct sales competition with the brand starts with the willingness to acknowledge and then fix those things that are unnecessarily frustrating the relationship. Following up with coordination and communication will enable retail partners to realize what a huge support component an ecommerce site truly can be for both of you.

Here are seven tactics to avoid in ecommerce that can frustrate relationships with retail partners:

1. Selling below MSRP

The highest margin sale a brand can make is direct to the consumer through its website. Brands that offer competitive pricing on their site along with other incentives can appear to undercut their partners. To avoid this, stick to MSRP for current-season and marquee products.

2. Not providing a store locator

Customers who use store locators on brand sites convert into sales 40% of the time. Not providing one or making it difficult to find or use guarantees a lost sale. This also affects the potential for all future sales to that customer. Support your brand and channel partners by providing a robust and easy-to-use store locator.

3. Making a site that works for the company not the customer

Too many brand sites feature content that is focused on the company (the history, the founders, the brand story, etc.) rather than the products. While it may seem like this focus keeps the site from competing with retailers, it is actually hurting everyone. Customers are looking to the brand site for detailed and helpful product information, and if brands are too busy talking about themselves, nobody wins.

4. Not coordinating promotions with retailers

Brands and retailers that coordinate promotions, win together. The opportunities are endless, and few companies are coordinating efforts in this way. Offering retailers a discount coupon for their customers and a kickback for the referral to an online sale is a great way to start.

It can get tricky for brands to avoid the appearance of playing favorites with retailers. One solution is to create SKUs exclusively for retail partners. This tactic is similar to creating exclusive products for the brand website.

5. Selling only a select portion of available products

Retailers feature the most current season's products, with last season's gear available on clearance. Customers are not always looking for the most current version of something, and may even be seeking products or parts that are difficult to track down at a retail location nearby. This provides an opportunity for brands to support both retailers and customers by offering their complete product catalog and replacement parts for sale online.

6. Not offering replacement parts online

An easy way to build trust and loyalty is to provide replacement parts and accessories in addition to an expanded catalog of services and support on the brand website.

When replacement parts or extended warranties are available for purchase directly from the brand site it makes life easier for customers and retailers. This is also a great opportunity to point customers to updated versions of a product or product line.

7. Limiting online marketing support to an AdWords budget

There are many ways a brand can support its online retail partners beyond marketing co-op dollars for cost-per-click campaigns. Unfortunately, most brands do not pursue them. It is up to brands to provide their partners with high-quality product images, content, and videos for use in the partner's marketing efforts.

This collateral support helps brands control how their products are displayed and marketed and helps both brand and partner websites with SEO. There are endless ways brands can support their retailers so that everyone wins.

Be creative in supporting retailers and improving relationships. Use targeted email campaigns or custom landing pages using brand content to get seasonal marketing messages out to the broader customer base of retailers.

STUCK POINT™ 3:

INSUFFICIENT SITE TRAFFIC

There are many ways to drive traffic to your site. You can be Amazon or Nike and people will come to you, you can wait and hope your latest SEO trick works, or you can go out and earn your traffic.

Of those three options, earning your traffic is the most work, but it is also the most effective way to drive qualified traffic to your website. Consider two effective methods to earn traffic.

Email

Email is both an incredibly powerful marketing channel and a consistent way to generate significant ongoing revenues for your brand. Of the hundreds of brands we have worked with to grow their online revenues, email was responsible for at least 5% of their total online revenue.

When a new product launches or is about to launch, email is a great way to queue up pre-orders and build buzz. When inventory of popular products is running low, it is easy to put together a list of products that are in stock and email them out to your customers to drum up revenues. Regular brand emails are a great way to stay in touch with your customers, providing multiple touch points that can be leveraged to generate revenue and optimize brand messaging.

Email list segmentation

Email marketing drives sales through promotional and transactional emails. It offers an opportunity to include a use case for each product in promotion, helping customers imagine the product in their lives.

Segmenting your lists will bear fruit in your email open rate, click through rate, and conversion rate. A simple segmentation you can apply today is recent customers versus new signups. Measure the effectiveness of each email sent to each segment to learn and adapt each future email.

Further segmentation and focused messaging can refine your email marketing efforts, making it a very profitable channel.

Paths to grow your list

There are essentially two ways to build an email list: buy a list all at once, or get people to opt in over time. Both can be quite effective.

If you choose to buy a new email list, there are services that will be happy to sell you one. Do not expect to see a high conversion rate from the list, at least initially, and absolutely expect people to drop off every time you send an email to that group.

Depending on the cost and the quality of the leads you receive, buying a list can be a great way to boost the size of your marketing lists immediately and add a few new customers.

Building an organic email list

The most valuable email lists are filled with engaged customers who are eager to buy your products and tout your brand to family and friends. The problem is that most brands are using a tactic to capture emails—the email pop-up—that is directly opposed to the type of site experience that drives engagement and sales.

Instead of helping the customer achieve their goals, the email pop-up that appears seconds after the visitor arrives on your site not only interrupts this process, it actually obstructs and annoys customers.

Defenders of email pop-ups point to metrics that prove that they are effective in adding addresses to lists. What is not as clear is the potential that those emails will belong to people who only joined to make the pop-up go away. They may be less likely to spend money on your site and more likely to click delete, unsubscribe, or worse, mark your email as spam.

Why not build a more valuable email list, filled with quality customers, using well-timed and well-placed email requests? Here are four ways you can:

1. Experiment with timing and placement of the email form

Timing your email request is the single most important factor in building a quality email list. A well-timed email request tells your customer you value their information (and time).

Proper placement of the request helps capture emails during

the natural course of your customer's visit, yielding quality email addresses.

To find the proper placement, first study how your most engaged customers are using your site and then put the email sign-up where you think they will be. For example, the bottom of a detailed product description can be a great location to place an email sign-up form. Customers who are digging into the details about your brand or a particular product are already interested in you, and they would likely welcome the opportunity to hear from you. Other placements to consider are in the footer, on the About page, or above the navigation bar. The sidebar is a common place for the email sign-up form, but it is often overlooked or ignored by customers.

There are even times when the pop-up may be appropriate, but only if that interruption occurs as a logical next step in the context of your customers' visit. For example, a customer who is spending time researching a product's specs and has been on the product page for fifteen to thirty seconds might respond positively to a pop-up that offers them the opportunity to receive more information. A purchase incentive in exchange for their email also works nicely.

2. Pay it forward with incentives

Before a customer is asked for any information, they should receive something of value. This could take the form of free shipping or an offer to save a percentage on their purchase. Paying it forward like this lets the customer know you value their time and is a way of acknowledging the value of the information you are asking of them. It also reinforces their perception of your brand's approach and commitment to greater customer service.

3. Ask for the email address at checkout

Most customers will provide their email to you at checkout so they can receive tracking information and a receipt. Do not confuse this with setting up an account, which you should make optional.

4. Include an incentive to sign up in the post-purchase follow-up email

When you send your customers their receipt and tracking information, offer them a personalized incentive to sign up for future emails such as an offer for future discounts, free shipping, or a percentage off their next purchase. This assumes your brand does not automatically opt-in customers when they enter their email at checkout.

Successfully growing your email list with quality email addresses hinges on your ability to seamlessly integrate the timely request into helpful experiences on your site. Interrupting the site experience with pop-ups or other distractions may add emails to your list, but the results those emails produce may not drive the results your brand is looking for.

Sending email

The most cost-efficient marketing tool your brand has at its disposal is email marketing. It is cheaper than almost all other marketing and advertising tools, it converts at a much higher rate, and it can be a primary driver of sales to your site. It can also easily be improperly used and abused. Here is how to do it the right way:

Provide something useful

The best email marketing is done by providing readers with something useful—a tip, a new way of doing something, or a bit of inspiration. By providing something useful within your email (or a call to action that prompts a click through to your site), you can dramatically increase relevant traffic to your site.

As a part of its email marketing, Snow Peak uses its Dictionary blog (dictionary.snowpeak.com) to inspire campers. The brand's ethos is all about inspiring people to get outside, and its blog champions that message.

Not every brand or agency can afford to go as far as Snow Peak does. Being helpful can go just as far. Shopify's ecommerce blog (shopify.com/blog) and related email marketing exemplifies being helpful without the content effort of Snow Peak. Shopify's tips and tricks for ecommerce websites are essential reading for anyone who runs an ecommerce site.

What puts Snow Peak and Shopify's email marketing in the best-in-class category is that, while their email marketing is designed to draw readers into their brand, the blog posts and related content are not about the brand; they are about the reader. By being useful, they build trust, authority, and good will toward their brands.

Keep the email simple

We all are bombarded with email offers every day. You might

be reading this book right now because of an email we sent you. (Thank you!) What sets apart an email that is opened and clicked versus one that is ignored, trashed, or filtered into spam? The answer is surprising: keep the email simple.

We have tested most methods of email marketing and found that by using plain text of two or three sentences in length and a link placed consistently in the second sentence, we get more opens and more clickthroughs than if we use splashy graphics, big buttons, or gimmicky subject lines.

By creating simple, direct emails, you will find that your email list will respond with more opens, clickthroughs, and conversions.

On those Buzzfeed headlines: Just because Buzzfeed says you should use headlines and subject lines like "Top 5" or asking provocative questions does not mean you should. Our most successful email marketing efforts come from subject lines that are directly related to the topic, not click-bait that sends the reader down a rabbit hole.

Be consistent

If you are expected to meet someone at a specific time on a specific day, you show up. The same protocol holds in email marketing. If your readers expect an email from you every week, send one every week. Changing the rules of the game can have a destabilizing effect on recurring visitors.

Emails should be consistent in their structure and signed by the same person. At The Good, our emails come from the same person every week, and this person's emails are short and to the point. He also receives all the responses, opt-out requests, and positive and negative feedback.

Consistency pays off. Our email marketing efforts have resulted in more qualified leads and increased conversions. We do not try to sell readers on our services or bombard them with offers; we consistently aim to provide useful insights to help them better serve their customers online.

Be polite

Not everyone will like your email marketing, and not everyone will opt-out in a cordial way. Regardless, be polite and respect their request.

If someone asks to opt out, opt them out

If someone responds to the email with all caps using foul language, do not take the bait. Politely opt them out and reply to their email request; this lets them know there is a human on the other side of the email marketing efforts and that you respect their wishes.

This polite treatment has actually led to a number of deep client relationships for The Good. You might be surprised what a personal email will achieve with someone who is upset.

After years of honing our approach, our content marketing efforts are essentially on autopilot. The heaviest lifting is researching and writing *Insights* every week. We divide that effort up among a few writers.

The effort has paid off. In the three-plus years that we have been writing *Insights*, we have seen our opt-in list grow from a few dozen to hundreds of thousands. Our open rates are 150%

above industry average, and our click through rates are 400% above the average.

Paid search

If you are spending more than you are making on paid search, your budget will be cut, and your online sales will drop. Driving traffic to your site through paid search is an investment game that sometimes requires a few losses to make many gains. There are a few variables in play that determine your ROI:

- Traffic generated (cost per click, or CPC)
- Conversion rate
- Average order value
- Lifetime customer value

The most commonly used search engine is also (not surprisingly) most commonly used to drive traffic through paid search. With AdWords, it is easy to think that the more you bid on a keyword the higher it will rank, and thus the higher it will convert. However, Google has come right out and said that conversion rates do not vary much with ad position (adwords. blogspot.com/2009/08/conversion-rates-dont-vary-much-with-ad.html).

Let us take a closer look at AdWords using your new bike helmet business, assuming the following variables:

- Cost-per-click bid on "bike helmets" keyword: $2
- Paid search conversion rate: 2%
- Average order value: $50 (with a profit of $25)

$$\frac{\$\,2}{\text{CPC}} \times \frac{50}{\text{VISITS}} \times \frac{2\%}{\text{CONVERSION RATE}} = 1\text{ SALE @} \frac{\$\,50}{\text{AVERAGE ORDER VALUE}}$$

$$\frac{\$100}{\substack{\text{COST TO ACQUIRE} \\ \text{1 CUSTOMER}}} - \frac{\$\,25}{\text{PROFIT ON SALE}} = \frac{\$\,75}{\substack{\text{NET COST TO ACQUIRE} \\ \text{1 CUSTOMER}}}$$

Based on these variables, it will cost $100 to drive 50 people to your site, resulting in one sale worth $50. This one sale profits $25. In the end, it costs $75 total to acquire one customer. This is completely unsustainable unless your lifetime customer value is greater than $75.

$$\frac{\$\,0.50}{\text{CPC}} \times \frac{50}{\text{VISITS}} \times \frac{2\%}{\text{CONVERSION RATE}} = 1\text{ SALE @} \frac{\$\,50}{\text{AVERAGE ORDER VALUE}}$$

$$\frac{\$\,25}{\substack{\text{COST TO ACQUIRE} \\ \text{1 CUSTOMER}}} - \frac{\$\,25}{\text{PROFIT ON SALE}} = \frac{\$\,0}{\substack{\text{NET COST TO ACQUIRE} \\ \text{1 CUSTOMER}}}$$

To break even on this ad campaign, the maximum amount you can afford to pay is $25. In order to drive those same 50 potential customers to your site (netting one sale), the maximum bid for "bike helmets" should be $0.50 per click instead of $2. This will lower your ad position on the page and may take you longer to generate 50 clicks, but with a 2% conversion rate, you'll break even.

Once you get to a breakeven point with your ad spend, you can begin to work on other variables like average order value and conversion rate to increase your site's profits.

Landing pages

Landing pages, also known as squeeze pages, are an effective way to maximize conversion and ROI on paid search spend. Simply creating ads and sending people to your homepage is a massive waste of cash. Instead, there are two opportunities to test and optimize conversion: the ad itself (copy, position, etc.), and the landing page.

The problem is that brands too often use landing pages for multiple objectives, blurring the goal of the page, sacrificing conversions, and wasting time and effort. To avoid this, you must continually test and optimize landing pages and ads in tandem.

The best landing pages have a clear goal and one call to action. By following a goal-oriented approach to landing page content creation and design, brands can keep the focus narrow and achieve higher conversion rates.

Know your goal

Before embarking on content creation and design, be sure the goal of the landing page is known and concrete. Without a well-defined goal, the landing page becomes useless to both the brand and the customer. For example, if the goal of the landing page is to gather emails, focus the content on enticing customers to provide their information to the brand via a simple form.

By knowing your goal, the landing page becomes a focused marketing and sales tool instead of another page consumers ignore. Increase the value of your time and the brand's site by keeping landing pages simple, with goal focused initiatives.

Know your audience

If you are trying to speak to everyone, you will reach no one. Each landing page should be focused on a specific goal to reach a particular audience. Obviously, the ad sending the traffic has to line up with the offering on the page. If the landing page is trying to sell soccer shoes to an audience of basketball players, the effort will fail.

Keep to the goal

The urge to insert hyperlinks and an abundance of distracting content on a landing page is powerful and must be suppressed. The goal is the only thing that matters. The brand's website can (hopefully) handle all the other stuff.

With the goal firmly established, create content that compels customers to accomplish the goal of the page (sign up, click a link, buy a product). Each element and word on the page must work toward the accomplishment of the goal. Save the details and distractions for blog posts.

Test

The nature of the web is one of fluidity and change. Gone are the days of set it and forget it websites that are only updated every two years during the next frustrating website overhaul. Instead, websites and landing pages are the testing ground for ideas.

The cost of A/B testing two different colorways on a landing page is a pittance compared to deciding in a conference room what the site should look like and making it the law. The web is littered with derelict conference room-approved ecommerce sites that harm a brand's reputation and lose an opportunity to serve and sell to customers.

By creating goal-focused landing pages and testing different messaging, design elements, and calls to action, brands can actually save money, convert more customers, and actively research and design future iterations of the brand's site.

There are a number of commonly used industry tools to assist in boosting landing page conversion. A few worth looking into are listed at thegood.com/tools.

A program for growth

Spending money on driving traffic to an under-performing site is a waste of your budget. You are better off using that ad budget to improve the conversion of existing traffic.

Once you have improved your conversion rate to a healthy level, shift your budget toward driving traffic. You will end up saving money and earn more revenue in the process.

Use the specialized calculator at thegood.com/tools to visualize the impact and ROI of prioritizing spending to grow traffic or conversion rate.

STUCK POINT™ 4:

POOR INVENTORY PLANNING

The final piece of the channel management puzzle is making sure there is enough inventory to sell online. Many brands struggle to manage their online inventory due to a lack of either the right process or technology to segment their products by channel.

It does not do any good to increase conversion rates and drive more traffic to a site that doesn't have anything left to sell. It is common for distributors to buy up a lot of inventory, especially of a brand's most popular products, wiping out online inventory.

Despite the fact that an online sale is the highest margin sale possible, many brands allow their retailers to purchase their entire inventory, without setting anything aside specifically for sale online. Further compounding this dilemma are aggressive online growth targets for online sales that are set without connecting the dots between selling more products and having more products to sell.

Inventory planning needs to account for all variables including marketing, site improvements, and just sheer luck. To plan for these variables, marketing and finance teams must synch up regularly during the year to ensure inventory planning is aligned with sales goals.

While inventory planning seems like an obvious tactic, many brands only realize during the busy holiday season that they have a handful of their top-selling products available for sale online, and it will take months to restock.

Real-time inventory management is a major roadblock to significant online sales growth, and brands need to plan for it or suffer from lower sales numbers despite high demand.

When everyone wants to buy, but there's nothing to sell

One client saw such a strong boost to sales through our Conversion Growth Program™ (thegood.com/program) that the client sold out of the firm's most popular product inventory within two months. Historically, the client did inventory planning on a semi-annual basis, so due to the large spike in sales it was necessary to wait nearly four months before additional inventory could be allocated to online sales. Fortunately, many potential customers asked to be notified when the products came back in stock, and the emails they sent when the products were re-stocked converted at over 40%.

After the products were back in stock and there was enough data available to estimate the opportunity cost of unavailable inventory, the brand had missed six-figure sales numbers while its products were out of stock. With our help, this experience led to a complete change in the way the client projects and allocates inventory for sale online.

The problem of growth

Ecommerce targets cannot grow unless departments within a company are coordinating their planning efforts. Growth is a good problem to have, but is unsustainable without planning based on what is happening in real time. The typical bi-annual planning for inventory impairs continual, year-round marketing efforts. This is a recipe for an unexpected revenue drop, unhappy customers, and missed revenue goals.

Investing in stock

An effective marketing strategy can change sales numbers quickly, but the lead time required to restock products remains the same. Brands cannot plan for everything, but there are a few key times that should trigger a fresh look at inventory forecasts.

Inventory planning triggers

1. Launching a new product

The buzz around a new product launch will draw new and interested customers. The extra traffic will likely result in extra sales of products outside the one just launched. Whenever a new product is launched, keep an eye on the stock levels of all popular inventory, not just the newly minted one.

2. Launching a new marketing campaign

Aside from the marketing push that goes along with a new product launch, there is the year-round effort to stay relevant to the brand's customers and to connect with them on a level that matters to them. If it works, the brand is going to sell more products.

3. Improvements to the site experience

When it is easier for customers to buy, they buy more, and they buy more often. Brands that are actually concerned with boosting online sales in a meaningful way are moving toward creating an experience that is simple and helpful to customers, or at the very least, not in their customers' way.

If your brand has made these kinds of improvements to the site's customer experience, you have likely noticed an increased number of customers who make a purchase on your site.

This increase in sales will directly affect the inventory available for online sales. Plan for it.

4. Keep your eye on the balance

To avoid retailers wiping out ecommerce revenue opportunity, segment your inventory for your ecommerce channel and your partner channel and commit to keeping it segmented. To avoid cannibalizing your own inventory, look regularly at how your efforts to drive direct sales are working out. If things are going well, you will probably need to order more than you thought you would.

Feedback about real-time sales numbers must flow through the company quickly enough to allow for the adjusting of inventory based on seasonal sales trends.

Planning is great only if the plan is agile enough to keep up with reality. Plan for future sales growth early so you do not go into your biggest season without the inventory to match customer demand.

Key outcomes checklist:

☐   Channel support strategy

☐   Traffic generation strategy

☐   Inventory management plan

Moving forward

How revenue flows into the brand can be as diverse as rivers flowing into the sea. It is no small task managing all channels while keeping partners happy, customers satisfied, and revenues up. Striking a balance, however, is vital to increasing online revenue. In the next chapter, we look at how site content can play a role in helping this balance.

4 | Content

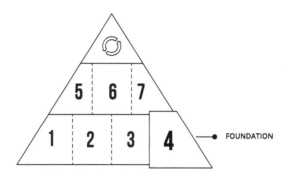

> **"** If you put out the best content and you are the best destination for brand representation, it is going to help all sales channels. Be true to yourself, and take the time to give the consumer what they need; everyone will win."
>
> Jenna Fallon,
> Global Digital Ecommerce Director at Yakima Products

Putting the right content online is the most important job of a digital brand manager. While there are often many internal departments fighting for space on the site, there are far more customers trying to fight their way through the site to find content that will help them make a buying decision. It all comes down to content that helps someone buy a product online.

According to the Nielsen Norman Group (nngroup.com/articles/e-commerce-usability/), about two-thirds of site visitors arrive with a predetermined goal. Of those, one-third of people search for a particular type of product without a specific product in mind. Another third look for a specific product. The final group visit simply to see what is available.

Visitors who arrive onsite via search are typically less loyal and less likely to purchase than users who navigate directly to the site. It is critical to help these visitors quickly find what they are looking for once they arrive.

The Nielsen Norman Group also reports that, while 39% of all customers come from search, almost two-thirds of search users abandon their first result to make a purchase elsewhere. In contrast, 71% of visitors who navigate directly to a brand site complete a purchase on site.

Thus, it is important to treat each visitor differently and support easy navigation through your site catalog, considering each of these customer goals:

- Specific item purchase (predetermined goal, intent to buy)
- Category research (product goal, researching with intent to buy)

- Bargain shopping

Stocking the shelves

Now that you are thinking of your site like a store, think of content creation as stocking the shelves with well-packaged products. Anyone can haphazardly throw together a thrift store-style arrangement of information, but it takes careful planning to craft an intentional online shopping experience through effective brand content.

It is easy to be caught in a cycle of simply putting content online and feeling like the work is done. However, the number of brand websites that have a product catalog full of poor-quality photos and badly written product descriptions far outnumber the brand sites that have taken the time to create purposeful online content.

This has nothing to do with creating a website that represents a brand well visually. Many brand sites look incredible, covered in beautiful rotating banners with epic slogans and brand storytelling videos to draw the user in. This content, however, is ultimately very shallow. It looks great, but it does not serve customers the content they seek.

These sites often have a section devoted entirely to all the video campaigns that the brand has put together. It is very unlikely, however, that any of those video campaigns are centered on helping a customer to understand a particular product better. It is far more likely that they have been designed to create a certain type of feeling about the brand itself.

It is fine to want someone to feel great about your brand, but remember that if customers are on your website, your marketing has already worked. You do not need to continue to market to them as if your site were a storehouse for commercials. Once they are on your site, it is time to sell them your product. This means that, while brand-focused videos are great, product-focused videos are even better.

Very few brands have set aside the time or budget it takes to produce quality supporting media for their products online. This is the new frontier of competition on the web. Brands have evolved from simply moving their print catalog online to supporting their products with better images. To compete online, they will finally have to invest in generating helpful product-focused videos.

Customers depend on web content to make purchase decisions. The importance of useful product content cannot be overstated. If the quality or the delivery of your content is poor, customers will let you know by not buying your products.

It might feel like an expensive proposition to create videos for each of your products. However, it is far more costly to miss millions of dollars in potential sales because your content cannot convert.

Let us look at a few ways to create great content, while staying focused on the highest ROI possible along the way.

OUTDATED AND POORLY MANAGED CONTENT

There is a sense of dread that fills brand teams (and digital brand managers) when they are faced with the task of auditing, updating, migrating, or moving content, especially from an old site over into a new site. Whether it is a content audit spreadsheet with 500,000 lines or a site with fifty products, moving and updating content can be an overwhelming chore.

This process does not have to be quite so daunting or painful because, with an eye on what people are actually viewing, you and your content team can reduce the total amount of work they need to do.

By limiting content audit, creation, and revision to the brand site's customers' top goals, products, and content, content creators can greatly reduce the overall scope of their work and focus on improving the most profitable parts of the site—the content consumers are actually using.

To do this, let go of the idea that everything on the site is essential. It is not. It may be important or serve a purpose, but if the site is designed to sell products or generate leads, then product and service pages that convert the most are essential, while pages that struggle to convert are not.

To sever this tie with the old way of managing, migrating, and auditing content, consider this analogy: when moving into a mansion, does it make sense to bring in old college furniture? There may be some sentimental items that make the migration, but the Goodwill couch and futon do not need to come. The same goes for your site's content.

Sever the ties with the past and be free for the future. Focus on the content of the top-viewed pages. Doing this first will provide a template for the rest of the site. Improve only those pages that time and resources allow, thus allowing the new (or newly revised) site to have content that is refreshed, relevant, and ready to help customers make a purchase decision. This will also free the brand's content team time to focus on top content.

In order to determine what this top content is, you will need to have a firm grasp on your site's analytics. Using the data that the site already has, the team can determine what products, pages, and content are actually used and which are not.

This abbreviated to-do list will help prioritize the content that needs immediate revision and improving and content that can exist without any revision (for now):

- Use analytics to uncover top content, goals, and products
- Conduct a content audit on the top pages (as determined from analytics)
- Create a page table for each page type based on existing content and new content needed
- Revise existing content and create new content for top products, content, and goals
- Leave the rest of content as is (this content will be revised later when time and budget allow)

Remember, the content you leave untouched is not going to live on like leftovers in the fridge; it will be dealt with in due time. Instead of trying to fix all your site content at once, focus on the content that does the most work for the site. Making your top content great will immediately improve your site's efficiency and productivity.

Having a shorter list of top products, services, pages, and content to revise or rewrite gives you the power to budget your team's time efficiently by ensuring the majority of their time is spent on the most profitable content on the site. Where you draw the line is up to you, but we have found that focusing on improving the most popular 20% of a site's content will do 80% of the work to see results. Efficiency and profitability equal a pat instead of a monkey on your back.

This model of content management is designed to create a more productive department and digital brand team. Content is not cheap to produce or easy to maintain, so finding ways to make the content you currently have work harder (and better) is essential. Once you have a template in place for the existing top content, creating content for new products as well as revising older content becomes easier and cheaper.

STUCK POINT™ 2:

NO PROCESS FOR CONTENT CREATION

Great content acts as a stand-in for a knowledgeable salesperson. It is a way for customers to guide themselves through your products. It allows them to compare benefits across product lines and between brands, and to choose the right product with confidence.

A clear outline of the performance-based differences between products, supporting video content, and user reviews will make it much easier for users to sort through your products. This kind of content allows customers to find something they feel confident purchasing directly from a brand website.

People will not buy from you if they cannot readily get all the information they are looking for. Success in online sales only comes when the right type of product information is available to allow the customer to sell themselves on your products.

Do not live in fear

The fear of leaving out a potential customer keeps many brands from creating content that will resonate with an actual customer.

Digital brand managers who want to get more action out of their online content need to make sure they have the right content online, and that means crafting and sharing content that is highly relevant to a specific, targeted audience.

The problem is that, too often, the organizational structure of the company ends up killing the right content. Consider the digital brand manager who knows exactly what he wants to say and to whom but who has to pass it by twelve different executives for approval first, each with a different agenda and point of view. This is a common process that ensures that what is eventually approved will not capture the interest of anyone.

This pecking order of disaster prevents digital teams from doing their jobs well and prevents customers from getting the service they are coming to the site for, frustrating both brand and consumer (www.smashingmagazine.com/2010/06/why-design-by-commitee-should-die/).

Here are three ways that digital brand teams can create and protect content that will resonate with customers.

1. Make it easy to imagine

There are plenty of reasons why someone might want to buy your products instead of some other brand's, but those reasons have less to do with features and benefits and more to do with the experience a customer is hoping to create (or avoid).

Always remember the main job your customer is hiring your products and services to do. Then show them how reliable, affordable, durable, fast-acting, loose-fitting, comfortable, comforting, or whatever it is your product or service is excellent at by helping the customer see what those things will mean for them. In whatever way your product will change the typical customer's experience, write about that.

Unless all copy, photos, and videos supporting your products or services make it easy to see how awesome life can be with your products or services, keep simplifying what you have until they do. Making sure everyone on your digital team is aligned with that purpose will enable you to accomplish the metrics-driven results the management team is after more easily. You cannot get ROI unless you invest in bridging the gap between your product or service and your customer's goal.

Ultimately, a brand's story is told by a happy or frustrated customer. The only way to shape that story is by providing support, value, and alignment around what customers care about, talk about, and share online.

When it comes to your site, stop making commercials. Use

your site to show customers how your brand can become a part of their show. When a customer is on your site, your marketing has already worked. Now it is time to help them with doing what they came to do.

2. Tell your customer's story

Brand story and customer story are the same. Brand history is another beast entirely. Do not confuse them. Any authentic brand story is one told by your customer about an experience they had in which your product or service played a part. Think about a surfer catching a perfectly shaped wave off the coast of Brazil or a rock climber making it higher than ever on a challenging route. Your product might be involved, but the story is not going to be about your brand.

Whether you are a content producer or digital brand manager, your job is to align any brand stories you tell with the stories your customer will be telling down the line: the problems solved, opportunities created, personal records set, times shared with friends and family, and so on. Do not let the "make the logo bigger" (brolik.com/blog/make-logo-bigger/) mindset take over your content; say less about the brand and more about what your brand makes possible for your customers.

Ask yourself if the storytelling on your brand site is obviously relevant to the goals of your customers or if it sounds more like a series of pointless anecdotes on a late-night infomercial. Remember that your brand site's main job is to show customers how your products will make their lives better, easier, happier, and generally more awesome.

Weaving your brand story into the content on your website (instead of leading with it) enables your brand to stay classy and relevant, making customer touches more efficient and effective. The real job of your brand story is to help your customer see how much more awesome their lives would be with your products in them.

Forcing your customer to wade through your brand-centric story does not bring them any closer. In fact, it creates a big obstacle to their purchasing goal. Therefore, since your goal is revenue generation, communicating your brand story in the wrong way is actually blocking your success.

Once the customers are there, use your brand story in a way that shows them how your products will enable them to pursue the adventure and achievement they seek, including stories about your brand they will tell for you, often for years to come.

Jargon-be-gone

We worked with a world-famous brand to rewrite their site's product technology descriptions from brand-centric marketing jargon to explain the tech in a way that relates the benefit directly to the customers' real-world experience with the product. That single effort instantly boosted conversion rates by over 20%. Jargon can sound cool, but clarity drives revenues.

3. Let your customers share the (real) details for you

Reviews, feedback, questions, photos, and videos from your current customers will all say more to your potential customers than you ever could. Ask customers who have previously purchased and experienced your product to tell others, in their own words, what it is about your brand that makes life better for them. This will enable potential customers to validate your claims. These customers may not believe everything you say about your products, but they are very likely to believe what your customers say. Use your brand's site as a platform to let your customers share the adventures, fun, relaxation, struggles, and victories your brand has helped them to and through.

The easy road is to sanitize all conversation around a brand and its products to only what is convenient for the brand. Because of how the human brain is wired, the shiny, happy people approach to product promotion can instantly kill credibility with today's consumer.

Super-relevant, targeted content can provide the kind of authentic connection with customers that will increase your opportunities to deliver the experience they are looking for, one that can only be had with your products.

On great content

When you put the right content in front of the right people in the right way, a few dollars can quickly build engagement and exponentially increase revenue. The main challenge is shifting the content focus from the brand to the consumer.

> **The opportunity now is for brands to build campaigns around what their audience wants to talk about, fostering advocacy in people whose friends will listen to them."**
>
> Sara Lingafelter, Director of Content Strategy at POSSIBLE

Storytelling for the sake of making the brand seem cool can have the effect of cooling customers from buying. Great online storytelling has to be about the customer and how their life will be better with your product in it. Customers do not visit brand websites to hang out and read brand story marketing. They visit to find out about your products and to buy. Placing unnecessary content in their way only reduces the chance that they will complete a purchase.

POOR QUALITY CONTENT

Quality content leads to a confident purchase. If customers can decide through photos, reviews, guarantees, and video that they should buy from you online – and 75% of shopping customers who watch product videos will buy (blog.kissmetrics.com/product-videos-conversion/) – they will.

Priorities for content creation

- Outline the key tasks and goals of your site visitors
- Highlight areas with the most potential for positive change
- Align customer goals with company goals

The following checklist provides a comprehensive framework for moving customers from evaluation to action.

Descriptions

- Plain English, jargon-free, unique to product
- Sell benefits not features
- Tell brand story with a product focus
- Offer clear product differentiation
- Explain what a product is best for
- Explain differences between products within a line
- Use *Read More...* for longer product descriptions

Images

- Multiple high-resolution angles or 360° views
- Detail level close-ups
- Product-in-use & lifestyle shots

Video

- Close-up product views
- Voiceover explains how to best determine proper size & fit
- Highlight unique product benefits, explaining choices within a product line
- Show people wearing and using the product; how do you wear, fit, apply, etc., the product
- Customer or celebrity testimonials

Sizing & fit

- Detailed charts for correct sizing
- Photos and videos of people wearing the product
- Sizing preferences based on performance need
- Will a different size provide better grip or protection?
- Is this product sized differently from most?
- What size should be ordered for comfort, sport application, etc.?
- How warm is the product?
- What features does this product have? (stability, compactness, lightweight, etc.)

Pricing & availability

- Always show pricing, even if MSRP
- Expected shipping & delivery times (offer free shipping if possible and display this offering prominently)
- If a product isn't in stock, direct customers to a nearby store

STUCK POINT™ 4:

LACK OF USER REVIEWS

Ninety percent of buying decisions are influenced by online reviews. Incentivizing the submission of user reviews after purchase will build brand value and customer community as they share their experiences with products, making it more likely that others will buy online in the future.

Sixty-three percent of customers indicate that they are more likely to purchase from a site that offers product reviews and ratings. This applies to negative ratings as well. A one-star review that explains why the product did not work for a consumer can provide context to a potential buyer for why the product may actually work for them. Often negative reviews stem from an issue with size or appropriateness for a particular activity.

If the review is truly negative, it also provides an opportunity for a brand's customer service team to respond in line with the customer. This demonstrates further trust and willingness to serve customers and is a great way to increase social proof.

Effective user reviews contain:

- Star ratings
  - Overall rating
  - Specific info on product features
- Reviewer qualifications
  - Age range
  - Descriptor
  - Skill or experience level
  - Favorite type of activity or use
- Description of pros and cons or likes and dislikes
- Explanations of how the product has performed for them personally

Testimonials and endorsements

Humans are drawn to faces, and when a testimonial appears online, without a face, it is received as inauthentic (and therefore ignored). However, put a face to the name, and the testimonial becomes truth.

Be careful with testimonials. Stay away from testimonials that use "great service" or "best ever" language. This is too generic.

Instead, use testimonials that describe a particular pain point and how your product or service remedied that pain. The closer you are to the pain points of your brand's specific consumer personas, the more effective the testimonials will be in converting sales.

STUCK POINT™ 5:

SOCIAL MEDIA INTEGRATION

Social media are powerful influencers, and brands should include link buttons to their social properties on their brand site. Those buttons should be in the footer, however. Using social buttons elsewhere can slow a site, distract customers from the purchase path, and reduce conversion rates.

Having said that, avoid social buttons with counters, especially on product detail pages. If a product has few likes, this tells the consumer that either no one is buying or no one likes the product (negative social proof). They will move on to choose a different product, or worse, a different brand.

To paraphrase Moz founder Rand Fishkin, when it comes to social counters, no proof is better than low proof.

Do not rely on social share buttons to make your content easy to share; focus on creating excellent content, and it will be shared. Here is why:

- Social media users know how to share content without using a share button

- Social share buttons often slow site load times and reduce content trust if share counts are low

- Social share buttons with a counter for the number of times a page has been *Liked* acts as a deterrent, especially when no one *Likes* the page or the product

STUCK POINT™ 6:

LACKING CONTENT OR FEATURES FOR COMPARISON SHOPPING

In our experience conducting user tests and interviews, we have found that users want to compare products side-by-side to figure out what will work best for them. After narrowing their choices to two or three options, they will compare every last detail right down to user reviews.

Over half the customers we have conducted tests with abandoned their session because they couldn't find enough information about a particular product to make a confident purchase. Detailed product information cannot be compared if it is not there in the first place.

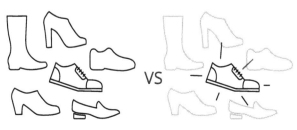

The best way to promote useful product comparison is to provide easily comparable information about similar products. Without this kind of information, differentiating your products from each other requires wading through a sea of marketing jargon.

Typically, when users try to compare products side-by-side, they will open links in multiple tabs and jump between them. We have even seen people put together extensive spreadsheets in an attempt to determine the best product, cataloging the smallest details. Some sites offer a product comparison tool, but comparable information is often not available even within these tools.

An excellent product compare tool:

- Provides the same kind of information about similar products
- Contains detailed technical specs
- Offers sizing tips based on performance needs
- Describes the best-use case for each product
- Helps customers choose between similar products within a series (basic, standard, pro, pro xl, etc.)
- Has prominent links for:
    - Removal or addition of items for comparison
    - Returning to a product detail page
    - Adding items to the shopping cart

THE FAQ PAGE

Getting user feedback is hard. It is so hard that companies pay war chests of hard-earned revenue to consulting agencies who wheedle it from their audiences. They drag "average Joes" into two-way mirror testing chambers, invade their most private social networks, and inject pop-up surveys between them and their content at every permissible opportunity, all in the name of finding out what is meaningful to them.

So you would think, if there were an abundance of voluntarily provided feedback, they'd treat it like some kind of godsend and react to it with equal parts compassion and excitement. Instead, we get the modern FAQ page.

Ninety-nine percent of FAQ pages are built with two kinds of BS: lies and laziness.

Let us set aside the inane practice of brands, inventing their own "frequently asked" questions (which are lies) and assume your customers are persistently barraging you with the same set of inquiries, day in and day out.

If people are constantly asking you the same questions, it means two things:

1. These questions are important to your audience
2. Your website is doing a poor job in answering them

Your website's customers do not want to contact you to get the information they need—that's why they are on your website to begin with. For them, reaching out is a last resort, and, for each that does, more do not even bother.

Of course, we cannot predict every single aspect of an interaction ahead of time, and users are bound to surprise us with things for which we had not planned. It is what you do with this information that matters. Shelving it away in a dark corner of your website is not a particularly great way to seize the opportunity.

Like your customers' resistance to reach out, it should also be a last resort for you to create a FAQ page. In most cases it is a cop-out, a white flag of surrender. Most FAQ pages are basically saying "We give up. There's no way to design this site to accommodate user needs X, Y and Z—let's just toss 'em in a catch-all bin."

So what can you do instead? Treat user feedback like what it is: a valuable list of potential improvements you need to investigate and, usually, adapt your site around.

Your website exists to serve the overlapping needs of the business and its customers. It exists in a continually changing social environment, and that change needs to be met with equally continuous internal calibration.

STUCK POINT™ 8:

STAYING RELEVANT

It may seem daunting to keep up, but quality content will always be at the foundation of sites with high revenues. Improving conversions begins by identifying with your customer and the experiences they have on your site.

Champion the perspective of your customer within your company, and support them in every way you can. Fight for better content, fewer features, less clutter. Pay attention to which content is helpful and which is not. Use every bit of data you can find to improve your customer's digital shopping experience.

Staying relevant is not just about participating in a social media conversation, it is about making your products and content approachable to your customers online. Focus just as much effort on improving current content as you do creating new content. Your sales numbers will reflect the effort.

Key outcomes checklist:

☐ Content audit

☐ Content strategy

Moving forward

Creating and continually improving content is a huge task. For brands that focus and produce consumer-focused content, the rewards are incredible.

Be mindful, though, that great content can fall completely flat without a solid technical architecture underneath. In the next chapter we'll look at how your site's technology may be preventing its true potential.

5 | Technology

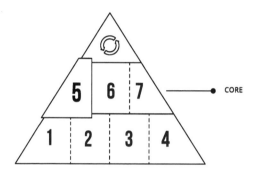

CORE

> **Success online is not about sophistication, it is about simplicity."**
>
> Nate Borne,
> General Manager at Snow Peak USA

It is easy to fall into the trap of thinking that technology (specifically re-platforming your ecommerce website) will boost your online sales. A new platform with more features can only be a good thing, right?

Wrong.

More features often get in the way of the very simple request a customer is making when they come to your site: Help me find the right product for my needs, and make it easy to purchase.

Re-platforming an ecommerce website almost always ends up including a rethink of the navigation, structure, content, and features of a site. In reality, those things can be done at any time, regardless of the ecommerce platform or a redesign schedule. Improving your site's experience and increasing conversions is about doing these things regularly, not just buying new features.

Technology is a prerequisite

If your customers notice which platform your site is running on, the odds are it is because they have run into a problem. If they do not, it is because you have invested in an acceptable baseline of technology (whether SaaS—Software as a Service—or self-hosted) that runs quickly and is easy to navigate and buy from. This puts you on par with every other mildly competitive brand out there.

So what are the most important components of a successful technology stack? There are a number of factors that allow your technology to contribute positively to online sales. We have also found a number of common roadblocks that keep your customers stuck and your revenues stagnant. Let's review both.

STUCK POINT™ 1:

A SITE THAT'S NOT RESPONSIVE TO ALL CONSUMER DEVICES

Unfortunately, too many sites still sit in the desktop-only ditch. As of late 2015, just 52% of the Fortune 500 companies have mobile-friendly websites. With technology for providing a quality mobile experience becoming cheaper (and easier to implement), more companies are making the move away from the pinch-and-zoom mobile experience toward a responsive web design experience.

About those m.sites

In the early days of the iPhone and the dying embers of the Blackberry, there existed a great new technology for helping brand websites show up on these new, tiny screens. These m.sites were great for helping brands bridge the gap between the desktop experience of their site and the mobile experience for their cool, hip, new mobile customers.

Times have changed, but for an alarming number of brands, their technology has not. With both adaptive and responsive web design now available, it is astonishing to see the number of sites that continue to provide a watered-down experience for their mobile customers.

With an m.site (and adaptive sites), brands are left managing two different sets of content on two different sites. Customers are forced to deal with an experience that includes less content and fewer features on one version.

Customers are not particularly keen on a separate, lesser site. If the consumer is coming to a brand site, they want the brand site, not an abridged version crammed into a standard mobile theme.

Responsively designed sites fluidly adjust to whatever screen size (and resolution) a customer is using to view the brand site, delivering the best experience for the particular screen. It also means only one set of content to manage and that the analytics reporting is unified under one URL.

Having a site that is not future ready is preventing it from reaching its full revenue potential. Making your existing site responsive is not just about making sure it shows up on mobile screens, but also ensuring it shows up on the next generation of screens, and then those released in the following years.

Lead generation sites are not immune from the ills of having a site that is not responsive. Your prospects and potential customers are using the same devices to view ecommerce sites. Serving up a subpar mobile or tablet experience to your potential leads tells those leads much about your brand's (in)attention to detail and value.

If your site is not yet implementing responsive web design techniques, now is the time to begin. If your company has not cared about creating a consistent experience across all devices, Google is providing plenty of incentive for them to do so now. As of April 2015, sites that are not mobile friendly do not show up in Google's mobile search listings. This is incredibly important to revenues because more than half of all web traffic comes from mobile and tablet devices, a trend that will only continue to increase over time. Go responsive or prepare to go out of business.

Numbers so good they seem fake

After we helped one client launch a new responsive design site, their mobile sales increased by over 650%. That kind of result can sound absurd, but it is real. After converting multiple brand websites from desktop-only to full responsive design, we've seen an average increase in mobile and tablet sales of at least 350% across the board.

If your site is not mobile and tablet friendly, you cannot afford *not* to invest in making it responsive. The longer you wait, the worse off you will be because Google now actively penalizes non-mobile sites in their search rankings. Do not forget, more than 50% of all web traffic now occurs on mobile devices.

STUCK POINT™ 2:

SLOW SITE LOAD SPEED

To maximize online revenue, your site must load fast. Ideally, your site's load time should clock between one and three seconds for both mobile and desktop customers.

On an ecommerce site that generates $1MM of revenue per year, every second the site takes to load equates to a loss of $75,000 in revenue per year (blog.kissmetrics.com/loading-time/).

What is surprising is how often site speed is overlooked. Many brands, content with the quickness of their homepage, forget that their product pages, category pages, and shopping cart's load speed matter just as much. Having a homepage that loads in two seconds is great, but if your shopping cart takes ten seconds to load (or worse, times out) you will lose a sale to another site.

Brands do not make their retail customers wait in long lines at registers, but they somehow seem to think it is okay online. Speed up your site; your customers will pay you for it (webperformancetoday.com/2012/02/28/4-awesome-slides-showing-how-page-speed-correlates-to-business-metrics-at-walmart-com/).

POOR SITE SEARCH

A site's search will play different roles for different ecommerce sites. Generally, the bigger the inventory, the more important search will become. Unfortunately, if there is one feature where sites consistently fail their customers, it is site search.

Customers who know exactly what they are looking for often turn to the site search with the expectation that this will get them what they are looking for faster than navigating through the site. Search terms customers use range from exact product names to product SKUs.

An excellent site search engine will:

- Return accurate and expected results
- Auto-suggest relevant keywords
- Account for:
  - Plural case
  - Singular case
  - Unique branded spellings
  - Category search (return product category listing page)
  - Common misspellings
- Offer helpful suggestions and top links on pages that return no results
- Provide visual results

Making search analytics work for you

If you have tracking for site search through Google Analytics, try this quick analysis:

1. Login to Analytics and navigate to: Content > Site Search > Top Queries > Export top 50 queries

2. Go through and test each query

3. Evaluate the quality of the results you find. To get started, categorize the search results into five main groups: excellent, good, poor, zero results, irrelevant

4. Measure how each of these search results compares to see how your site search is performing.

If you do not have site search set up in your analytics program, you can usually get the same data by identifying the first URL query string parameter when a search is made. If this is the case:

1. Go to your site and perform a search

2. Look at the URL in the address bar and search for a phrase beginning with "/search" such as /search?q=SEARCH-TERM

3. Go into your analytics program and navigate to Content > Site Content > All Pages > Search for your unique parameter

4. This will list all the pages that include this parameter in the URL

5. Export the data

6. Clean the data by removing all parameters and substituting dashes for spaces, etc. Once the data is clean, you are ready to evaluate the search quality using the previously mentioned methods

STUCK POINT™ 4:

TRACKING NOT SET UP PROPERLY

Most brands have some form of data tracking in place. There are a number of different platforms available for free or pay that allow you to track customer interactions on your website easily. Two of the most commonly used in each respective category are Google Analytics and Omniture.

Because basic Google Analytics is free, it is the most widely used, so it is what we discuss most often in this book.

Despite how easy it is to set up, not everyone has taken the time to turn on ecommerce analytics within Google, which allows the tracking of purchase conversion, and the monetary significance of other behavioral events.

Complete event tracking

Setting up basic tracking, including ecommerce tracking, is essential to making use of any site data in an actionable way. Basic tracking only provides a high-level overview of what's going on. To get real, actionable data requires a few more steps.

Event tracking adds another layer to the mix. Event tracking allows you to dig much deeper into customer behavior on your site. You can measure any kind of interaction from button clicks to PDF downloads, and sort them into four areas:

1. Category: Typically the object that was interacted with (e.g., button)

2. Action: The type of interaction (e.g., click)

3. Label: Useful for categorizing events (e.g., nav buttons)

4. Value: Values must be non-negative, useful to pass counts (e.g., 4 times)

Event tracking allows you to take a much more meaningful look at what is happening on a page. Instead of being stuck looking at time on site and bounce rate, you can have some idea what people are actually engaged with on your site at a page level.

Once all tracking is set up, use Google to run experiments with features, content, and navigation. These experiments will allow you to increase your revenues significantly while learning what works and does not work for your customers.

The trouble with numbers

When it comes to tracking ROI on a digital project, there's a frustrating lack of consensus on accepted metrics across projects. Because of this, it can be difficult to establish success metrics with which decision makers in your company will be comfortable. (The irony is that established formulas for tracking print media and PR projects are still simply estimations.)

Without easily understood metrics, many digital efforts wither on the vine. Many of the metrics that prove or disprove the effectiveness of a project are not something that can be simply pulled from Google Analytics or Facebook without first understanding customer and brand goals for the project. So that is where you need to start.

Answer these questions to find the right data to track:

- What is the goal for this project? For the brand? For the customer?
- What available data will prove or disprove the success of this goal?
- What actions along the path to goal completion will demonstrate success or failure?
- At what point will I know if this project has been a success or a failure?
- If the project is a failure, what lessons can be learned?

PLATFORM LIMITATIONS

Many companies struggle with the limitations of a legacy platform. Either there are multiple brands within a company that must share the same platform, or an internal IT department has set up a complex web of spaghetti code that only they can maintain.

There may be long-term contracts in place with a current vendor, or it may just seem too difficult and costly to re-platform. In any case, it can be a struggle to work around a legacy system to create a site that meets the expectations of today's consumers.

When re-platforming is not an option, check to see if it is possible to update the front-end code, the part of your site that your visitors interact with. This, at least, will improve the overall experience without needing to replace the technology behind the website.

Fighting for budget to re-platform is difficult, but it's a battle that will greatly improve the site's efficiencies. It will help foster a better customer experience, making lead generation and sales more efficient. It will help your team be more efficient by providing a user-friendly CMS to implement content and site changes quickly. Additionally, it can make inventory management more efficient by consolidating all inventory lists into one place.

Selecting a new platform

Despite the time and expense that goes with every re-platform, it can occasionally be worth it to ditch the limitations and frustrations of legacy platforms and move to a more flexible, modern solution.

When the time comes to decide on a new platform, many factors need to be taken into account. As you weigh your options, be sure to consider each of the following items:

- Average cost and platform revenue model (subscription, percentage of sales, etc.)
- Optimal SKU count
- ERP integration options
- Localization
- Current clients on system
  - Client revenues
    - Less than $1 Million
    - $1-10 Million
    - $10 Million+
  - Customer reviews of the platform
- Built-in CMS
  - Quality & ease of use
  - Flexibility to create unique content
- Partnerships with third-party developers
- Fulfillment partners and ease of integration
- Level of documentation provided for development
- Level of customization required
- Average time to set up and get started
- Expected total implementation time

- Maintenance requirements
- API and plug-in availability

Out with the old

Old thinking, old technology, and old platforms keep companies from moving forward. Legacy systems, integrations, and old ways of doing things die hard. In a perfect world, everyone would be better off simply starting over; exporting the old metrics and reporting data, and moving to a fresh, lightweight, cloud-based system that forever frees digital departments from the slow-moving politics of internal IT departments.

Old technology is crippling. If your company's progress is being held back by legacy systems, it is better to cut the cord and start over fresh as quickly as possible. The time and cost involved in integrating new systems with old systems are not worth it. The only thing you really lose when moving on from an old system is the past reporting data. These can be exported and saved for future reference. Do not let legacy systems hold you back from helping your customers.

INTERNATIONAL SITES THAT ARE NOT ECOMMERCE ENABLED

Not every brand sells internationally online. Brands that ignore the revenue potential of foreign markets risk missing out on a significant source of additional revenue. Brands that do sell internationally, but do not have ecommerce set up for those regions, are preventing customers who visit the site from enjoying an easier way to buy.

Hiding pricing

Many companies with international representations set up different localized versions of their site in the languages of each country or region. This is great for helping customers access your content and products. However, on these same localized sites pricing may be hidden or removed. As a tactic, this is OK, but hiding pricing has its drawbacks.

Hiding the pricing of the US version of Yourbrand.com from a customer in the UK or Thailand has negative SEO implications. In particular, Google discourages companies from hiding pricing in real time from customers, which is the only way to achieve this result. The risks are not worth it.

International dealers often have a problem with their customers being able to look up USD prices for the same products that they sell at a different price. From inside your brand, it may feel incredibly important to be sensitive to dealers' concerns about international pricing visibility. However, customers outside the United States understand that prices vary across borders, and for them it is much less of a concern. Adding an international dealer locator can also help in this regard if you receive a significant amount of international traffic to your domestic site.

We do not want to tell you how to deal with your international partners, but we do want to ease your fears about customer behavior regarding price. The most important thing is providing a consistent brand experience across all versions of your website. Create a high-quality experience with helpful content available in all languages, and support your customers in their research and purchase process regardless of where it is taking place. That is how you win more customers and make your dealers happy.

STUCK POINT™ 7:

TOO MANY TRACKING PIXELS

When it comes to website data tracking, too much of a good thing can become a bad thing.

For every tracking tag (i.e., tracking pixel) on a site, the site has to load that pixel from another server so it can do its work.

Over time, this accumulation of tracking pixels will cause the site to slow to a point where it can affect the revenue-generating capability of a site.

What is a tracking pixel?

A tracking pixel uses third-party services to collect data you can use to improve your site.

Tracking pixels earned their name from the original method of tracking site visitors by loading a transparent 1 pixel image. However, most service providers now use JavaScript to collect the information.

Some common services that utilize tracking pixels (or JavaScript) include Google Analytics, Omniture, CrazyEgg, SeeWhy, DoubleClick, Google AdWords, Certona, ChannelAdvisor, and MediaMath.

Duplicate functionality

Many tracking pixels that brands use are actually gathering duplicate data.

Pixels that monitor scrolling or generate heat maps are great for short-term testing, but implemented full-time they only duplicate data generally gathered via Google Analytics or Omniture.

The best advice is to use heat mapping and other performance anchor pixels during key testing times like new page rollouts or after a site redesign. After testing is complete, turn off tracking, and remove the associated tracking pixel from the site while keeping primary analytics tracking code in place.

What can you do?

There is a limit to the amount of data that is useful before it becomes overwhelming. There is also a limit to how much site performance (and revenue) a brand is willing to lose to gain duplicate data. To help moderate the epidemic of tracking pixel creep:

- Use only what you need. Accumulating a mountain of duplicate data only creates a dearth of insight and analysis. Will you actually be able to consume all of the data points, analyze them, and make changes because of them? There are diminishing returns when the data set becomes overwhelming.

- Load pixels after the page loads, and load the pixels all at once. A good developer can assist with this best practice.

- Use intensive pixels only as needed, such as right after the launch of a major redesign.

- Secure your data (via https) to ensure security vulnerabilities are plugged.

STUCK POINT™ 8:

TOO MANY ERRORS

Errors are the dirty underbelly of a website that nobody really wants to think about. Unless you are in the IT department, it is unlikely that you are aware of them at all. Errors can affect your site in multiple ways, all of which reduce the quality of your customer's experience.

The most common errors you may be unaware of are 300 errors (link redirection) and 500 errors (server or code issues). In both of these cases Google will penalize your site, making it more difficult for people to find you online.

Other common errors that are easily found by customers but often overlooked by brands include 404 errors (page not found). There are surprisingly many brand websites with main menu links that lead nowhere or on site search engines that produce zero results, which is (to the consumer) the same as a 404 error.

For the most part, unless your homepage or product pages aren't loading, it is unlikely that you'll find out about any of these errors on your own. You have to know where to look, and, once you find them, you have to be willing to invest in fixing them.

There are a number of free services available on the web to search your site for broken links, missing pages, and other server errors. Screaming Frog (screamingfrog.co.uk) offers a free SEO spider tool that will help you pin down all kinds of site errors.

Key outcomes checklist:

- ☐ Responsive website design
- ☐ Speed optimization
- ☐ Site search optimization
- ☐ Robust tracking setup
- ☐ SaaS platform
- ☐ International site support

Moving forward

Your ecommerce platform, CMS, and feature sets have little inherent value. They are the price of admission to get in the game. Good technology is now the baseline, and optimizing the consumer experience by reducing all of your brand's online sales killers is the way to victory.

Does running an ecommerce platform require some technical skill? Of course, but will the platform, CMS, or technological feature set help to double your sales? No. It is how you use technology that will allow you to double your online revenues.

In the next chapter, we will look at the customer path and how you can put all the Stuck Points™ together to create a website that exceeds brand expectations and delights your customers into buying your products.

6 | Customer Path

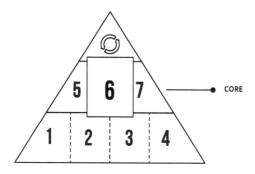

CORE

> If someone comes to your site through an entertainment portal, what right do you have to try to switch them into commerce mode? Same goes for research, you'd be crazy to shove a sponsored athlete video in front of them and lose the sale."

Chris Harges,
Director of Global Marketing at Mountain Hardwear

The path a customer takes through your website tells you everything you need to know about how to improve your site. Customers beginning their journey on your homepage advance through category level pages to product detail pages and ultimately through checkout. This may not all happen on a single visit, but the important thing to notice here is that none of these pages include brand-focused navigation or content. They are purely focused on the research and purchase process.

The fact that every brand website has much more navigation and content than is required for this path is bad for business. It means that companies have the wrong priorities for their websites. It means that companies are focused on themselves instead of their customers. It also means that both the company and the customer will end up frustrated.

If you want to increase your online revenues, you can do all the brand storytelling and content creation that you want, as long as it is all positioned along the customer's journey through your site and aligned with your customer's goals.

STUCK POINT™ 1:

BRAND EXPERIENCE VS. CUSTOMER EXPERIENCE

We are frequently asked, "What is the difference between a good brand experience and a good customer experience?"

It is simple. There is absolutely no difference between a good brand experience and a good customer experience. Your customer experience is your brand experience. The easier your site is for your customers to navigate from landing page to checkout page, the better the experience is, the better your conversion rate will be, the better your revenues will be.

Site management

Most digital brand managers have to be jacks of all trades, making it difficult to do well in specializations that they have neither the time and nor the expertise to master. Dealing with rapid change in the market landscape is hard enough when that is all you need to focus on, but since one person is usually responsible for multiple tasks, it is difficult to keep up.

Because things are always changing, lasting success is not about tools or technology. It is about a process that is focused on continual improvement that is based on and incorporates the results of small experiments over a long time.

STUCK POINT™ 2:

INFORMATION OVERLOAD

It is tempting to put up persistent links to everything on your site. Exposing every kind and category of content to users in one place seems like a great way to save people time. The problem is that most sites do not have the right content in the right locations in the first place.

More content means more to navigate through, more to search, more to manage, and more to keep current. Content maintenance becomes unsustainable and content quality diminishes throughout the site. Product descriptions and imagery become stale, videos lose relevance, nobody replies to questions, and sales drop as a result.

To avoid this, a consistent effort is generally needed to reduce the amount and types of content that are accessible online before addressing navigation.

For example, during a site redesign for a client, we discovered that the top 50% of the client's SKUs accounted for 80% of their revenue, while the bottom 25% of products accounted for less than 5% of total revenue. By focusing their content efforts on top-selling products, the client was able to reduce their workload, streamline their content, and increase overall traffic and sales on their new site.

Even with a reduction in the quantity of content, the site must still make the sale. To do this, your customers need to find the right products, and they must be able to assess their choices intelligently.

Build the right features

Based on the ubiquity of pop-up email capture forms, rotating image carousels, social media feeds, and brand story videos, it is easy to see that brand sites are copying each other. Rather than creating unique and innovative solutions to help their own customers with their specific problems, most brands choose their site features by looking around at what the competition is doing, assuming it is working, and recreating it with a new look.

"You know, make it like insert-iconic-brand-here," has been

heard in meetings at design agencies around the world. Most agencies shrug and comply, continuing to pump out the same epic-looking nonsense that gets in the way of what people are trying to accomplish. It is easy to point to companies like Apple, Nike, Patagonia, and Starbucks for inspiration.

Recreating a competitor's tactic on a website, especially without understanding the thinking and lessons behind that tactic, can lead to dangerous results. Results that diminish your own customer experience, and result in higher bounce rates and lower conversion rates.

Know your role

The web is transforming from a series of interlinked pages to something entirely different: a series of interactions that may or may not take place inside a web browser. As technology continues to evolve, it is increasingly important that each company intentionally designs digital interactions specifically for the needs of its customers. As this shift continues to take place, an associated shift in mindset and process is required to keep up.

The first phase of this shift is understanding that a customer's journey through a website has nothing to do with the way a company is organized. Many websites today simply reflect the way a company thinks about its own organization, and its site navigation and content bear witness to this fact.

Taking the time to organize and curate content around the way a customer interacts with your website will pay massive dividends. It may not be immediately popular internally, however, as multiple departments fight to keep their voice on the site. Fortunately, the purpose of a company's website is not to keep internal departments happy. It is to attract and convert more customers. That path is illuminated by examining the paths your customers take through your site.

Making features that align with customer needs

To design site features that will align with customer needs, start with two things: the right goals and the behaviors that will lead to the accomplishment of those goals. From there, you can design the features that support the behaviors your customers can perform to accomplish their goals.

Because it can be difficult to think outside the realm of features, ask questions designed to lay a foundational understanding of the site that does not include features. The resulting list can then be prioritized and reduced to just the main items. Even if you have unlimited resources, it would still be best to focus on designing the top three features perfectly versus designing a hundred features poorly.

Key to the iterative approach we have outlined is asking "why" and being genuinely curious about the answer. It is also important not to hold any answers too sacred to keep yourself and your team open to better solutions or to solutions that do not already align with your expectations of what should exist on your site in order to be successful. Your goal is to create a site that serves others, not just your company. Shifting the focus to your customers will help your team to engage in fewer debates of opinion and instead turn to testing for validation of ideas. The ideas that will win are the ones that help your customers the most, not simply the ideas of someone with the highest title.

Begin by establishing the main objectives of your site. Goals are not guesses, but pretty much everything else is, until you validate it with your users. You do not want to waste your time doing work that does not provide value or turns out to be a poor investment. This is why all your goals should align with what your customers are trying to accomplish, rather than simply what your company is trying to gain. Goals define your ideal outcomes for the site, while behaviors are measured for relevance and features for efficiency.

Here is a highly compressed overview of the path from goals to implementation:

Goals [Define] (Key stakeholder approval before build, validated internally) Goals set up behaviors to be validated, but do not need to be validated themselves.

- What do we want to get out of the website?
    - What problems do we want this website to solve?
    - Since we've launched this website, we've seen a (difference) in/of (something).
        - » Could add qualifier of "by _____."

Behaviors [Align] (Make sure what you want people to do is actually what people want to do, validated by users) Behaviors need validation. Highlight hypotheses and validate them through data analysis, user surveys, and user testing.

- What can we help people do to achieve this? (multiple possibilities)
  - How can the website be a catalyst for these goals?
  - What can the website do to support a goal?
  - How well does x behavior support y goal?
  - Make sure the result of an action points to underlying goal.
- Help (people) do (action).
- Qualify all guesses before building on them, by attaching a KPI/decisive metric to track.
- Determine relevance to brand and goals.

Features [Refine] (Possibilities, not prescriptions) Explore multiple options here. If your goal is "sell more event tickets," a calendar feature may not be the best method.

- How can we facilitate this behavior?
- How well does x component support y behavior?
- How well does this component help a user accomplish something, act, behave, etc?

Implementation is the actual process to support the

above items. Here your task is to diagram "the why," so it can be shared across teams. This prevents the need to diagram deliverables around "the what" because ultimately the what is your website itself.

- Align goals with supporting behaviors and their associated features.

- Determine how you will track conversions by behaviors.

- Prototype solutions that can be tested with users before launch.

- Launch features to small segments of your traffic for testing using traffic-splitting software.

- Track the effectiveness of each feature against your previously established KPIs.

STUCK POINT™ 3:

CUSTOMER UNKNOWN

It is vital to keep in mind that customers will access your site from a variety of devices in a variety of locations. Understanding who your customer is, how they are accessing your site, and what the primary goal of their visit is (by device) can mean the difference between a sale or an exit.

Many customers start their research and shopping on their phone. They may continue on their laptop and finish on their tablet. Brands that offer a seamless single digital experience across all devices will win by helping their customers towards a purchase decision with a great experience from wherever they are shopping.

According to Google (thinkwithgoogle.com/research-studies/2012-zmot-handbook.html):

- 77% of television viewers will use another device while watching TV
- 81% will use a smartphone while watching TV
- 66% will use a smartphone and computer at the same time
- 66% will use their laptop while watching TV

This multi-screening behavior will only increase as smartphone and tablet use increases, furthering the need for brands to be available when their customers come calling.

When customers are in a store, they will be looking for different content than if they were just learning about how to use a new product. Keep this in mind when creating and organizing content.

When it comes to site design, content should be prioritized by how likely it is a customer is in research-and-purchase mode versus looking for product support. Evaluate your customers' browsing paths by device so you understand how to prioritize content in a way that will be most helpful to each customer.

STUCK POINT™ 4:

THE OLD FUNNEL

Brands that cling to the traditional sales funnel mentality are at risk of being left behind by brands that embrace a single digital experience strategy. This strategy is not limited to the devices that consumers use. It requires a commitment to:

- Learn how your customers are using your site, anticipate their actions, and look outside your industry for ideas.

- Resist the urge to borrow ideas from competitor sites lest you unwittingly copy an ineffective idea that you perceive as good because you have seen it used over and over.

- Make your site responsive. Responsive web design will allow your site and its content to work on any size screen.

If you are in a rush to get your content right, promote content that your customers are using and products they are buying, and demote content that is not used along with rarely purchased products. This aligns your customer paths with the content they are most likely looking for. If you save your customers time, they will be much more likely to spend their money with you. If you waste it, you will lose the sale.

STUCK POINT™ 5:

COMMON FEATURES THAT ARE ACTUALLY ROADBLOCKS

Email pop-ups

We have already covered how to avoid the email pop-up as a way to build your email list in Stuck Zone™ 3: Channel, but it is important to make the point here as well. When you greet customers with an email pop-up, it is exactly as if they had walked into a retail store and been greeted by someone holding a clipboard offering to send them more email.

This tactic assumes that the number one thing people are trying to do when they arrive on your site is somehow to find a way to make sure you have their email address. It is annoying for the customer. Stop it.

Rotating carousels

This tactic is ground zero for herd mentality web design. It is hard to find a site that does not employ at least one rotating carousel. Despite the ubiquity of this tactic, it is not very effective in generating clicks.

According to multiple studies (thegood.com/insights/mom-called-hates-homepage-carousel/), static (non-rotating) homepage carousels are clicked by only 1% of a site's customers. Of the 1% who chose not to ignore the carousel, 84% clicked the first position, while the remaining four positions were clicked an average of 4% of the time.

Carousels that automatically rotate do not fare much better than their static counterpart. Rotating carousels averaged a higher overall use (8.8% click rate), and the first position still dominated with 40% of clicks. The second and third positions saw almost none.

What explains this horrible click rate for carousel banners? Several factors are in play:

- Banner Blindness: customers are so accustomed to the bombardment of daily advertising that they will instinctively look below the banner, often completely ignoring whatever is in the carousel.

- Poor Readability: not all of your customers read at the same rate or level. Slower readers may not finish the content on an automatically rotating carousel before it changes positions. International customers may also need more time to read the content.

- It Is All Just Advertising: carousels look like advertising, and when they automatically move, they look even more like a bunch of ads. While advertising works, it also annoys people, and if a customer is already on your site, do you really want to risk annoying them?

- Herd Mentality: Brands have a tendency to follow each other's lead when it comes to digital tactics, and this is one tactic that just is not helping anyone.

To break this trend in recycling old and unhelpful tactics, we have come up with four ways you can quickly make better use of the space currently occupied by your carousel and maybe start a trend of your own.

- Top products: know what your top products are and put them on your home page. If your customers are coming to your site and buying softball bats, have softball bats on the home page. This will save your customers time and instantly improve your sales.

- Top content: for sites whose customers really dive into content (or you have a product that naturally produces a ton of great content), display that top content on your homepage so your customers can quickly get it.

- Combination of top content and products: try different combinations of top content and top products to see which perform better. This will help you understand what is and is not working so you can do more with your precious space.

- Current promotion for that period: this can be helpful

during the holiday season or that time of year when your customers are looking for particular products you sell. Again, this requires that you actually know what your top-selling products are during those promotional periods so you can accurately display the content your customers want.

While there is a bit of experimenting to see which tactic works best for your site, what is clear is that the homepage carousel tactic does not work well. While we cannot hope to end the use of carousels on websites entirely, hopefully you will get your brand off the merry-go-round.

Brand-focused navigation

Sites with clear navigation are naturally accessible, guiding customers from landing pages through checkout. Not every page has to be accessible from the main navigation. The solution to an overloaded navigation is to put the main paths your customers are taking through the site right up front and hide the rest.

A quick look at analytics will reveal that the typical paths through your site are something along these lines:

- Home > product detail page
- Home > product category page > product detail page
- Home > informational page

Creating a site structure that better represents the paths customers are actually taking through your site will go a long way toward reducing premature exiting from your site and increasing conversion rates.

Study your site analytics to find the top paths your customers are using. Then take an honest look at your site's navigation system to see where the two are misaligned.

A CONVOLUTED CUSTOMER PATH

Once roadblocks are removed, your customer's path to conversion is that much easier. But just removing the barriers is not enough. To fully realize your site's potential, the following elements of your website need some attention.

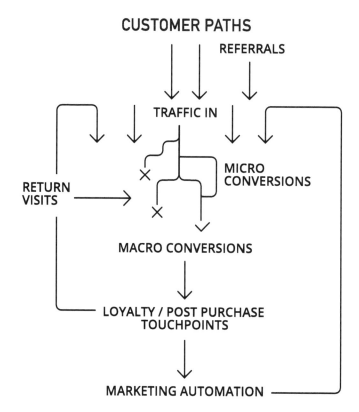

Landing pages

Every page on your brand website is a landing page. Whether it is designed as a specific campaign landing page, a product detail page, or a bio of the CEO, if it is on the site it is a point of entry for your customers. That means, if the page is not optimized for conversion, you risk losing a sale.

Using analytics to identify the top entry pages is a solid first step to ensuring that the content on those pages is positioned to maximize conversion. Here is some key content those pages should look to incorporate:

- Links to top-selling products
- Featured product videos
- Descriptively named product categories, prioritized by popularity
- Product search bar
- Store locator
- Customer service contact information
- Link to shopping cart

Landing pages that are simple to navigate and complete a goal have higher conversion rates.

The big impact of small changes

In working with a B2B client who had a 6% lead conversion rate on their product detail page, we incorporated some of the Conversion Growth Program™ product detail profiling best practices. This led to a conversion rate increase of over 300%. We further increased conversions through a series of small changes that better complemented user behavioral patterns discovered through testing.

To be effective, brands need to maintain a discipline of continual testing, iteration, and refinement to drive results. Small changes that align site content and calls to action with customer goals can have a massive impact to the bottom line.

Product category page

One of the most common landing pages for PPC is the product category grid. It is also the most likely location for your customers to end up on after arriving at your homepage.

Common features of the product category grid include filtering systems to shop by brand, color, size, rating, and price. The goal of the category page is to get your customer to the product detail page as quickly as possible. Ideally, time spent on this page should be low.

Customers tend to open multiple tabs from this category page to allow them to compare similar products side-by-side quickly. Offering a product compare tool feature can be helpful here, providing the contents available for each product are actually comparable.

Another key to a successful product category page is using high-quality images that all have the same aspect ratio and a consistent photographic style. Mixing lifestyle images with flat shots or knock-out backgrounds with products shot in a rich environment creates visual noise that is difficult to sift through.

Keep the top of this page scannable with brief, useful information. The most important information to show is:

- Product name
- Product image
- Product price
- Product rating

Design based on customer behavior

We launched a product filtering system for a client that sold similar-looking products with a broad range of prices. In this situation, a filtering system is typically an ideal solution. Rather than filtering by the qualities of the product, we created a filtering system based on the needs and qualities of the customer. The highly technical nature of the products made a customer-centric filtering system extremely effective.

Based on our research for this client, we knew the system would be helpful to customers. However, when we initially launched the filtering system, it was only used in 5% of all purchases. After user testing revealed that the design of the system made it blend in too well with the rest of the site, we made a series of visual design updates that ultimately resulted in 85% usage.

It was easy to get approval on the initial visual design because it matched brand guidelines perfectly, but customer behavior patterns ultimately determined (and should always determine) the most effective design. This is a great example of the results that can come from a brands' maintaining a continual testing mindset.

Product detail page

We covered the content for an ideal product detail page in Stuck Zone™ 4: Content, but, to summarize, an effective product detail page contains the following:

- Plain English, jargon-free, descriptions unique to each product
- Multiple high-resolution images that show people wearing and using the product
- Product-in-use and lifestyle videos that highlight special product benefits, explaining choices within a product line
- Detailed charts for correct sizing
- Pricing, even if MSRP
- Stock availability with an option to be notified when available if out of stock or an option to buy locally
- User reviews that contain star ratings, pros and cons, and a brief descriptions
- Tech specs that are comparable between products, and an appropriate level of detail to help customers research products across brands
- Expected shipping and delivery times
- Warranty information and registration

Store locator

No matter how good an online shopping experience may be, there will always be customers who feel more comfortable completing their transactions in a retail store. This makes store locators that are easy to find a necessary component to any ecommerce site, especially because 90% of customers who search for a store nearby take action within twenty-four hours (blog.hubspot.com/blog/tabid/6307/bid/24082/9-Amazing-Mobile-Marketing-Statistics-Every-Marketer-Should-Know. aspx).

A successful store locator:

- Is easy to find in the main menu and on product pages
- Is easy to use and includes key contact information for each store
- Provides directions from any starting point to a store's location

Helping your customers cross the finish line begins and ends with getting out of their way. Reduce the number of steps they must take to accomplish their purchase, and watch your conversions and profits increase.

Checkout

Sales and conversions cannot be improved without an optimal checkout process. Your site can be full of excellent content and still lose the sale at checkout.

Generally, the fewer fields your customers are required to fill out, the greater your checkout conversion will be. This applies not only to checkout, but to form design in general. The less people have to work to progress, the further they'll go through your conversion funnel. Removing just two fields can improve a form's conversion rate by 20% (conversionxl.com/53-ways-to-increase-conversion-rate/). One major ecommerce site found that by removing the register button (thus allowing for guest checkout) earned them an additional $300 million per year (www.uie.com/articles/three_hund_million_button/).

A seamless checkout process

If it is difficult to buy something from your site, people simply will not. Some of the most frequent problems that we see on brand sites could be easily prevented, especially at checkout.

The checkout process is ripe with opportunities for testing and improvement. Keeping an eye on this process means more than just looking at your cart abandonment rate. It means going through the process of ordering a product from your own site regularly enough to see where the process breaks down. It means looking at which products are added to the cart most often without resulting in a purchase. It means capturing customer email addresses earlier in the process so that you contact them if they do abandon their purchase.

Here's a list of best practices to help ensure your checkout process is as smooth as possible:

- Prioritize guest checkout
  - Offer an unobtrusive account login option
  - Provide an optional account registration *after* purchase is complete
- Preserve information
  - Recycle and pre-fill information submitted by customers whenever possible
  - Prevent information loss after a page

refresh, validation, or navigation error

- Request information efficiently
  - Auto-fill as much information as possible
  - Use geolocation to select defaults intelligently
  - Request zip code, auto-populate city & state
- Use billing address as default shipping address
- Clearly denote required versus optional fields
- Provide persistent form labels
- Display errors in-line, with descriptive text to help correct the error quickly
- Organize form fields in a linear vertical flow
- Provide clear calls to action; remove calls that do not advance a customer through the process
- Offer customer service contact information prominently throughout checkout
- Provide warranty and return policy information
- Leave opt-in fields (newsletter, social follow) unchecked by default
- Break the checkout process into logical steps and clearly indicate progress, as such:
  - Order summary
  - Payment information; calculate tax and shipping costs accurately
  - Shipping information
  - Order confirmation
  - Multiple payment options
- Prominently display security information, especially near payment entry fields
- Allow use of browser back and forward buttons

POOR CUSTOMER EXPERIENCE

No matter how amazing and memorable your brand experience is, it is the customer's experience that determines the success (and potential future growth) of your site. There is ultimately no difference between the brand experience and the customer experience. The two do not have to be permanently misaligned.

User testing

A little empathy for the customer goes a long way toward endearing them to a brand. Understanding the ways your customers interact with your site can reveal many obstacles to a purchase. The lessons that come from seeing what it is like to shop online with your brand can turn into the richest and most resonant brand storytelling yet.

An investment of a few hundred dollars here will pay for itself multiple times over by helping you to see where people are getting confused, distracted, or otherwise losing their patience with what feels to the brand like a slick and well-constructed ecommerce site.

Turning bad stats into good tests

Pages with high bounce rates, low conversion rates, or unusual data are prime candidates for user testing. Choose a handful of poorly performing pages, send testers to those pages, and assign goals you expect your customers to perform on those pages.

Some generic goals for user tests that you can make more

specific to your brand and products include:

- Find a product and add it to the cart
- Use search to locate a particular product
- Use the product filters to locate a particular product
- Add multiple products to the cart and attempt to check out
- Find support information for a particular product
- Attempt to make a product return
- Find answers to common questions about a specific product

Carry the momentum forward

Whatever you learn in a user test can be leveraged immediately. Track the results of the changes and assemble a library of data and lessons that can be leveraged well into the future. Use the lessons and data to measure the performance of new features and pages. This testing data will also help make it easier to argue for or against internal discussions about the site using real-world examples.

Optimize for success

In addition to user tests, live site testing can be an extremely effective addition to your toolkit. There are a number of services like Optimizely, Monetate, and Google Content Experiments that allow you to test almost any change or variation on your site to see how it performs against a specific goal.

These tests help you observe and assess small tweaks to links, wording, colors, and positioning of items on a page to compare how that change performs against the baseline. This is much less personal and anecdotal than a live user test, but the results are indisputable.

A few examples of site optimization tests to try on your site are:

- Display ad URLs (testing site.com/product-name versus site.com/product-category/product-name)
- Home page images
- Headline text
- Navigation bar display
- Navigation item order
- Button size, color, shape, and placement
- Button calls to action (placement and text)
- Site-wide calls to action (placement and text)
- Form field length and number of fields
- Page messaging and content
- Product pricing
- Reduced shipping costs or free shipping
- Mobile web page length

Splitting these tests up by new versus returning visitors can produce some interesting results. The simple beauty of these tests is that they are small and manageable. The lessons learned can be implemented immediately or filed away until time and budget allow.

Personalization

Site personalization is becoming popular as the technology becomes cheaper and smarter. Using data from past interactions with your site, you can provide returning visitors with a personalized digital experience, similar to something that might happen in real life.

Imagine going into your local coffee shop for the first time, ordering a favorite drink, leaving, and enjoying the beverage. On the next visit, the barista remembers and confirms the drink ordered yesterday; you are not just another face in the crowd. The next visit, the barista starts making your drink and it is ready by the time you get through the line to pay for it. What feeling does this create?

Just as a barista can have a profound effect on how welcomed a customer feels by simply remembering preferences and prior purchasing habits, a website can be a place that builds context with customers to remember their preferences and build a relationship with them.

The technology and data exists to provide a customized customer experience. Unfortunately, it is extremely rare for ecommerce sites to utilize the data that is readily available to accomplish this.

The key to providing a tailored experience is to display products and recommendations within a context relevant to the returning customer. For example, if the customer purchased a jacket on a recent visit, the website should not try to sell another jacket. Instead, offer the customer complementary products (e.g., gloves, hats, pants).

Additionally, as customers add items to their cart, the website should default to display items matching the size and colorway preference of items in the cart (or previously purchased).

Site search is another area perfect for personalization. Your website should track product searches and provide content around those products.

Focusing on the top search terms (for all visits) will also help identify which products and product categories should be promoted, discounted, or recommended to other customers. The aggregate customization data will allow you to adjust the site to surface automatically the top 20% of searched products and content to the key landing pages.

Facebook is a good example of using these technologies to tailor consumer experience. By implementing these technologies, Facebook better understands what types of ads should be displayed as users navigate around the Internet based on the way they use facebook.com.

When a customer makes a purchase, they are telling you with their money what they like. This is the loudest that a customer can speak to a brand—it is clear feedback on the products the customer wants. However, even before making a purchase, your customers are signaling what products and information they want; paying attention and tracking these signals will improve your conversion rate and significantly improve conversions on future visits.

RAISING THE BAR

Consumers expect an experience that is equal across all the devices, and their expectations will only continue to rise. To create the lasting relationships needed to improve your brand, you must not only meet your customers' basic expectations, you must delight them.

Delight is a natural emotional response to a site that is efficient, helpful, and beautiful. If your site were a restaurant, delight is the response to a meal and atmosphere that create a lasting memory and makes your customers want to come back over and over. Meeting expectations is competently served fast food. Delight is a well-thought-out fine dining experience.

Delight is the sliding scale through which expectations are eventually set. As companies innovate and provide more helpful and delightful experiences for their customers, those experiences will become the expectations your customers will have of you.

Key outcomes checklist:

- ☐ Customer experience optimization
  - ☐ Customer-centric organization
  - ☐ Customer-centric content
  - ☐ Clarity on customer intent by device
  - ☐ Prioritize content by popularity
- ☐ Remove tactical roadblocks
- ☐ Purchase path optimization
- ☐ Customer experience optimization
- ☐ Personalize and delight

Moving forward

Refining the purchase path to maximize conversion is often the final thought in increasing site revenues. There is, however, one more component to keep customers coming back—the post-purchase follow-up.

7 | Post Purchase

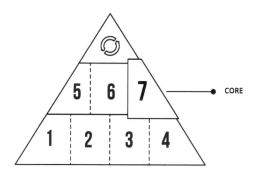

CORE

> **Digital is more about authenticity than anything else."**
>
> Lauren O'Connor,
> Senior Marketing Manager at GU Energy

A strong customer recommendation is better than any advertising or marketing effort. Capturing and promoting these recommendations is more important than ever on your brand website.

Your customers are sophisticated shoppers with a sensitivity towards obviously branded content. Often, the key to making a sale is not more content that the brand thinks its customers want to hear, but the authentic voice of other customers on the site. Providing opportunities for current customers to review and recommend products on your site is one of the most valuable tools at your disposal.

Many companies are too focused on acquiring new customers, and have either forgotten about or are completely ignoring the value of retaining their current customers. It is far more economical to grow current customer loyalty and increase their lifetime value than to focus exclusively on acquiring new customers. For this reason, it is important to stay in touch with your current customers and do everything you can to keep them happy.

STUCK POINT™ 1:

FAILING TO MEET CUSTOMER EXPECTATIONS

Every customer wants to know that their order has gone through properly and when they should expect their new purchase to arrive. This provides another convenient touch point where you can recommend other products, offer newsletter sign-up, and incentivize future purchases.

Many brands miss the opportunity to do this right. By leaving default ecommerce system email templates in place, they miss an opportunity to create another consistent, branded touch point. They also miss out on a chance to incentivize and gather more customer reviews on their products.

It is important not to overuse the ability to contact your customers via email. If you put the right touch points in place, you create a great experience makes it more likely not only that your customers will continue to buy from you, but also that they will recommend your products to others as well.

To keep your customers informed without overwhelming them, we suggest the following email contact structure:

- Account confirmation (if created)
- Product stock notification (if requested, when available)
- Purchase confirmation (upon purchase)
- Shipping confirmation (on ship date, with tracking number included)
- Post-arrival setup and usage help (on day of anticipated arrival)
- Post-arrival review request (one to two weeks after arrival)

If you look at product reviews on Amazon, a certain percentage of them are always purely based on the delivery and fulfillment aspect of the customer experience and have little if anything to do with the product itself. Provide the basics, post-purchase, to meet the basic expectation of your customer and reap the rewards.

The most important strategy around which to align your standard follow-up touchpoints is to address the questions and expectations of your customer before moving onto the ones that matter most to your brand.

MISSING OPPORTUNITY TO BUILD LOYALTY

Once a product has been delivered to your customer (or a service delivered), it is now time to keep the fires burning. Returning customers spend on average four times as much as new customers. To stay at the top of a customer's mind, or at least visible in a crowded arena of brands, you must keep in touch.

> It is critical to bridge the worlds of automation with a human touch. Set up touch points to ask questions, and let customers know what's going on and what will happen next. That's where loyalty begins."
>
> Travis Nagle, Owner at Viesso

Request a product review

Customers are happy to share their experience with the product, whether good or bad. If their experience is extreme in either direction, they will certainly share their opinion without any incentive at all (although incentives work well, too).

It is important to consider your audience in your post-purchase follow-up. Most customers already understand how to share their experiences online and will do so without much prompting on your part. Your job is to make it as easy as possible for every customer to share their opinion.

Depending on the type of product or service you offer, the timing of your review request email will vary. If you sell an experience, it is probably best to follow up two or three days afterwards. If you sell a product that might take a little while for them to use, wait two to three weeks before requesting review.

The email you send should be clear and direct. The subject line should also be direct. For example, "Review your purchase of product name from company.com." Including an offer for a discount on future purchases or a personal share link to offer that same discount to their friends once they have posted their review will go a long way to generating responses. Be creative, and offer value in exchange for someone taking the time to help you sell more products.

From 30 to 3,000

After launching an email campaign to request product reviews automatically a few days after each purchase, one client saw their on-site customer reviews jump from just 30 to over 3,000 within six months.

It is not enough simply to ask for the review; you need to learn what will ultimately incentivize the most people to offer their opinion for others to see. This is where running multiple campaign tests and quick iterations to learn what resonates best will serve you well.

Send a survey

We have already talked about how surveys are a great source of actionable data for your brand in Stuck Zone™ 2: Customer. A post-purchase survey is an excellent way to learn how you can better serve your customers online. This approach may not make sense for every brand, or for every product sold, but when used properly it can create significant value.

The most important thing to remember when you send out a post purchase survey is to ask questions for answers you care about and can act upon.

Potential survey questions to try on your site:

- How did you find us?
- Why did you buy?
- Did you have a good experience?
- What could we do to improve?
- Are you happy with your purchase?
- Would you refer us to a friend?

A discount with a deadline

People like discounts, especially from their favorite brands. But this tactic should be used with caution. Too many discount offers can breed inaction and diminish urgency. However, offering occasional discounts with a deadline can drive huge spikes in converting traffic to your site. These are great to use at the end of a season or during a lull. A well-timed email with a strong offer with a deadline can generate sales quickly.

Upsell related products

If a customer likes what they bought from you, they may also buy a related product you recommend. Recommending a product or service related to something your customer has already purchased is a great way to provide value to the customer and generate additional revenue in the process. Just make sure the recommendations are relevant.

Ask for a social follow

While this tactic is not particularly important to your customer (because it offers them no value unless your social feed has great content on a consistent basis), it can be an effective way to boost social followings.

For this tactic to be effective, the email should be very clear about why someone should opt in to follow your brand online. If you are not consistently and frequently doing something unique and powerful with your brand's social media presence, do not waste this touchpoint. Your customers will quickly perceive you have nothing to share and are just wasting their time.

Loyalty points

Creating an effective customer loyalty program can be a difficult undertaking. If you are going to implement a loyalty program, the key is simplicity.

If your customers do not have to manage another account, and can simply earn points associated with their email address, they are much more likely to cash in any points they have earned when you reach out to them via email with an offer to do so.

This tactic is only for brands ready to commit to creating

a valuable loyalty program that is continually tested and improved over time. Until your brand is ready, stick to the basics and create a great customer experience worth repeating.

Keep following up

Email and content marketing is a great way to connect with your customers and to offer them exclusive deals and incentives that drive traffic and build loyalty. Restraint is always advised to avoid oversaturation.

Many brands miss the opportunity to leverage their growing email list. There are often so many other priorities that it is difficult to plan and manage a successful post-purchase campaign. Brands who manage this well will see about 5% to 15% of their online revenue come through the email channel.

Key outcomes checklist:

☐ Optimize post purchase touchpoints

☐ Build lifetime customer value

Moving on

Following up with your customers post purchase may help drive sales, but the frequency and relevancy of the follow-up can lead to customer burnout and decreased conversions.

By fully understanding your customer and testing each touchpoint, you will turn your post-purchase follow-up into another healthy revenue channel for your brand.

Conclusion

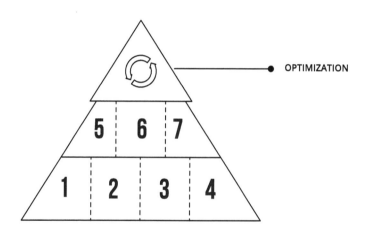

OPTIMIZATION

We believe the launch
is only the beginning."

Shaun Tinney & Jon MacDonald,
Partners at The Good

The best way to leverage the tactics we have covered is to put them to use consistently through a process of ongoing testing and optimization. With a continuous effort to improve customer experience, it is inevitable that you will grow revenues and build a playbook of repeatable ways to increase sales.

From projects to process

There is a disconnect between people and the numbers they represent in analytics. For every bounce, page view, and conversion there is a person completing those actions. Often, in the course of a busy day/week/season, we forget that, when a bounce rate increases or conversion slips, our sites are failing a person who visited with the intent to accomplish something.

It is hard to empathize with a number; there is no emotion when looking at statistics that rise or fall. Many decisions we make on our websites are based on this emotionless analysis of numbers. This is a mistake. It takes constant reminding that those numbers represent people (and potential customers).

When you check out at retail stores, a cashier typically asks if you found everything you were looking for. This does not happen online. The personal connection is missing and hard to replicate. In lieu of trying to empathize and serve our customers, we take the calculated view of our visitors that replaces them with symbols. Instead, we need to see our customers for who they are—people who are trying to do something *important to them* on our websites.

To correct this calculation, start with the idea of one person.

It is much easier to think about helping one person find what they are looking for than helping ten thousand. By beginning with one person, we begin to see where our sites fail, succeed, or just chug along. We can begin to rate our site's experience as either good, neutral, or bad. We stop only focusing on the numbers, and we begin to empathize. This change in mindset creates better sites, better experiences, and better revenues.

To help you make this shift, we will outline a process similar to the Conversion Growth Program™ we use with our clients (thegood.com/program). Beyond all else, this iterative program is designed to get you thinking about that one customer, and then expand it to all customers. It is also a way to stop thinking of your site as a *project* on a two-to-three-year redesign cycle and to start thinking of your site as a *process* that leads to constant improvement.

The result of this program is a site that delivers for your customers and, as a by-product, the content and functionality of the site itself.

Continual redesign versus continual improvement

You would not plant a garden and expect anything to grow without tending to it. The same is true on the web. Too many brands invest their entire digital budget on a brand new design every few years, only to find the new site is just as ineffective as the last.

Instead of constantly making new sites (and spending

your entire digital budget in one shot), spend your digital budget, over time. Focus on speeding up your current site one month, improving product content the next, improving search performance the next, and working your way through incremental improvement (navigation paths, category names, product images, ratings, and reviews). Each of these gradual improvements will add up to higher conversion rates and revenue. They will also save you from having to rebuild your site every few years.

This process of continual improvement involves tasks like:

- Ensuring top-selling products are easy to navigate to
- Testing and evaluating the site's search results for top onsite search terms
- Evaluating page cost and value beginning with important pages with high exit rates
- Updating and removing old or ineffective content
- Running user testing on the most common customer paths to ensure ease of use

By implementing this process for clients, we have consistently seen performance improvements in all areas—in some cases, sales have increased by over 900%. The payoff is absolutely worth the effort, and it is a much safer bet than spending your entire budget on a new site.

This continual focus on improvement is the only way to get an actual return on your digital investment.

Conversion growth

The strategies and tactics covered in the previous chapters build toward two goals:

1. A solid foundation for a powerful and lasting digital presence

2. A process for sustainable growth

The first few Stuck Zones™ establish the elements required to fund and build your brand site properly, providing clarity around your audience and the strategies required to understand and serve their goals. These foundational elements should be evaluated periodically for efficiency and cohesion with your brand goals do not need to be addressed on a monthly basis.

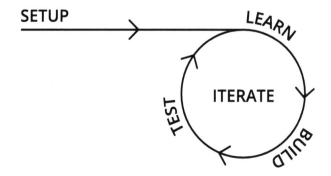

Once you understand, clearly, who your site is for and how it will help them, and you are sure you have chosen the right platform on which to run your site, it is time to focus on conversion growth. This monthly process will help transform your site from a brand-centric, revenue-light site to a customer-centric, revenue-heavy site.

There are no easy answers here, but the process is designed to surface the right answers for your brand through quick testing and learning cycles. This process of trial and error will ultimately replace the process of bi-annual site redesign, by replacing those large guesses (and investments) with a series of smaller ones stretched out over a long period of time.

Conversion growth checklist

To prepare your site properly for an ongoing growth program, first make sure that the foundational pieces are in place. Once the foundation is laid, it is easier and far more efficient to implement the conversion growth process elements.

The following highlighted items from the chapter checklists create the foundation for a successful site:

- Correct funding for your site
- Clear vision and brand goals
- Clear customer goals
- Traffic generation strategy
- Content strategy
- Responsive web design
- Robust tracking setup

Once the foundational elements are in place, you can then

focus on conversion growth through:

- Customer-centric site optimization
- Purchase path optimization
- Customer experience optimization

Common roadblocks to growth

Once a site is launched and a conversion program is running, there are a number of things that can seriously reduce the momentum of growth. These roadblocks primarily fall into two categories: company and content.

1. Company roadblocks

Limited buy-in from management

If your management team does not understand or agree with the process of trial and error as the only path to real understanding and revenue growth, it will be difficult to implement a conversion growth program fully. Limited buy-in usually results in smaller budgets, an inadequate number of resources for your team, and a lack of commitment to customer-centric site improvements.

Inventory and stock issues

It seems pretty straightforward, but this is so common it must be reiterated: you cannot sell what you do not have. Through this process of constant testing, we have seen conversion rates improve so quickly that online inventory will sell out by summer, leaving nothing for the holiday season. It is critical that inventory projections are regularly updated and stock is properly segmented based on current online sales trends.

Ad spend consistency and growth

If you are spending to drive traffic to a site with a poor conversion rate, much of that money is going to waste. If you are spending time increasing that conversion rate, the ROI on your ad spend will consistently increase. That extra revenue should be continually reinvested to keep the whole funnel growing. We have seen brands cut or reduce their monthly ad spend as a means of saving money and then wonder what happened to a large percentage of their online sales. Do not do that, or, if you do, do not be surprised when the sales drop along with your ad spend.

2. Content roadblocks

No site promotions

Running regular promotions through email to drive traffic to specific landing pages and changing out the content on featured promo areas on your homepage are essential to keeping things fresh. This requires paying regular attention to your content strategy, evaluating what is working and what is not, so you can build a revenue-generating playbook. When you know that running a shipping promotion to boost your average order value will generate an additional $10,000 in monthly revenue, you will know where to turn when you need to grow sales.

No personalization strategy

Personalization is the future of the web, and most sites are not even close to providing a personalized experience to their customers. When everyone sees the exact same promotions and content regardless of whether they have visited before, filled out their information, or made a purchase, tons of opportunity is left untapped.

No content updates

A stale site is just that. The effort required to speak with your customer service team to find ways that site content can be improved is minimal. The impact of that effort is massive. Take the time to uncover the top issues your customers run into, and find ways to clear them up with better content and organization.

Next steps

Do something. That is the next step. Do not allow your site to idle for another day. Proactively test and optimize your site. Learn analytics, understand what your data is telling you, test content, test calls to action, strategically move content around the site, get rid of your carousel: do something. The alternative is not an option.

Improving your site's conversion rate is not as easy as simply paying more money for ads to drive traffic, but the payoff is far greater. Work on making your site work for your customers first and then spend the extra revenue to drive as much traffic as you can afford.

Where it is all headed

Digital has evolved from its primordial days of thinly disguised brand billboards with flashing Christmas bulb borders. We have moved past the "Isn't it cool, we have a website" phase to a new phase in which digital is in every part of our lives. From phone apps to touch screens at the grocery checkout, it can be nearly impossible to avoid a digital interaction during the day.

From this always-present digital presence, we have evolved as well. We now expect automation, personalization, and self-service. We do not want to talk with a store employee, we want to do research on our smartphone. We do not want to stand in the line at the grocery store, we want to use self-checkout (or use our phone apps to have groceries delivered). At the airport, we prefer kiosks to clerks. Digital's influence is everywhere and touches all parts of our lives.

One place that digital still lags behind is on the web. Our websites still subscribe to the antiquated idea that the sites exist to promote ourselves and our brands. This is wrong.

As customers have come to expect self-service everywhere, the websites we build and run need to provide customers with what they expect and demand. And what they demand is clear: a website that serves *them*. Anything less is a failure.

This service has many qualities, but the two most important are helping customers quickly research and purchase products and providing a personalized experience.

Helping customers research and purchase products quickly is

the first priority of any ecommerce site. Without first attending to this customer service, all other tactics and strategies will ultimately fail.

Personalization is the future of the web

Providing a personalized experience is the next phase in serving your customers. Personalization is the future of the web, and it can be had now. Start by serving returning customers with the content they previously viewed or complementary products for past purchases. Progress to remembering their preferences and size, and go from there.

Personalization is not difficult to implement, but it can be hard to implement right. It requires a dedicated approach to customer-first web design and content creation. It requires attention to analytics and the will to make changes that the data tells you to make. It requires using your website to be like the barista who remembers your coffee order every morning and serves it to you without having to hear your order.

Websites that remember and serve their customers with personalized content will emerge as the true champions of customer service, and will have the increased revenues to show for their efforts.

The choice now is before you. Do you choose to remain sitting in the cave watching the shadows on the wall, or do you turn around and take action? Do you keep your site focused on the brand, or do you make the changes that will keep your site and brand profitable well into the future? There really is only one right answer.

What next?

Growing conversions online is an art and a science, and it takes constant effort to achieve strong results. We are here to help if you are stuck or need help in improving your site's conversion rates.

If you are managing the process yourself, be sure to check out thegood.com/tools to download checklists and other resources to help you along the way.

If you need help and want to increase online conversions dramatically, visit thegood.com/program to learn more about our Conversion Growth Program™.

Thanks for reading. Here's to a better Internet for everyone.

About The Good

The Good is an ecommerce and lead generation advisory that helps brands exponentially grow their online sales. We've spent years developing, testing, and improving methods to increase conversion rates and grow revenues online. In recent years, brands that have worked with The Good have seen an average revenue increase in revenue of over 100%.

Learn more at thegood.com.

About The Authors

Shaun Tinney is a Partner and Director of Research & Strategy at The Good. Since joining The Good as a partner in 2010, Shaun has led development of the revenue growth process that consistently delivers strong ROI for The Good's clients. In addition to leading the research and strategy for The Good, Shaun frequently writes and speaks to help brands reach their sales and service potential.

Jon MacDonald is Founder and President of The Good. As President, Jon has helped lead the firm to become one of Oregon's top 20 fastest growing private companies. Jon volunteers for several causes throughout the Pacific Northwest and is an active committee member of industry associations and peer groups such as Entrepreneurs' Organization (EO).

59640456R00110

Made in the USA
Lexington, KY
10 January 2017